The
Hard-to-Teach
Child

The Hard-to-Teach Child

A
Diagnostic-Remedial Approach

Denis H. Stott, Ph.D.

Formerly Professor of Psychology and
Director of the Center for Educational Disabilities,
University of Guelph,
Ontario

With contributions from
A. E. Brown, M.A., Ed.D.
Marie J. O'Neill, Ph.D.
George O. B. Thomson, M.Ed.
Leonard F. Green, M.A.
Sidney Brown, M.Ed.
Jean Francis, M.A.

University Park Press
Baltimore • London • Tokyo

UNIVERSITY PARK PRESS
International Publishers in Science and Medicine
233 East Redwood Street
Baltimore, Maryland 21202

Typeset by The Composing Room of Michigan, Inc.
Manufactured in the United States of America by
Universal Lithographers, Inc.,
and The Optic Bindery Incorporated.

Library of Congress Cataloging in Publication Data

Stott, Denis Herbert.
The hard-to-teach child.

Includes index.
1. Learning disabilities. I. Title.
LC4704.S76   371.9'2   77-25005
ISBN 0-8391-1175-4

Contents

Guide to the Chapters

CHAPTER ONE notes a widespread dissatisfaction with 'deficit' concepts and the resulting labeling and inappropriate treatment of children. Despite the universal concern, our educational systems still fail to provide effective follow-ups on early identification.

A description is given of a demonstration project in schools under the Toronto Board, the purpose of which was to work remedially with educationally high-risk children in order to prevent the risks becoming actuality.

CHAPTER TWO shows how the concept of 'intelligence'—the most notorious of the hypothesized deficits—has blinded us to the realities of mental development and in particular has penalized the socially disadvantaged.

The notion that children have 'learning disabilities' can be equally pessimistic. We should think in terms of non-use or poor use of capabilities rather than in terms of disabilities or deficits. The latter concept has neither stood the test of research nor provided teachers with clear guidelines for understanding and correcting learning failure.

CHAPTER THREE proposes an alternative concept to explain individual differences in mental development and educational attainment. It is based on the developmental theory of mental growth recently advanced by several leading thinkers in the field of learning.

Mental growth is seen as a function of experience, the structuring of experiences into concepts, and putting concepts to work in the form of thinking skills. In accord with use or non-use of the mind, growth or retardation is cumulative. The theory emphasizes the open-ended nature of capabilities, rather than limitations of potential.

CHAPTER FOUR extends the developmental theory to the motivation of thinking and learning. The most important motivation, hitherto little utilized in education, is the child's feeling of enhancement that arises from being competent and effective. Effectiveness-motivation, so termed, rewards those mental activities that favor mental growth—making discriminations and generalizations, the gaining of understanding, and the acquisition of problem-solving skills.

A deficiency of effectiveness-motivation, seen as unforthcomingness, can result in a developmental retardation. An excess can cause behavior problems and learning difficulties.

CHAPTER FIVE deals with assessment. Standard tests are misleading because they are founded on the concept of limited capacity, whereas the operative variable is the degree to which the child uses his capabilities. Belief in IQ scores may discourage attempts to improve mental functioning and condemns the child to continuing retardation.

The main target of assessment should be to measure improvability. This can be done only by working with the child in a program of diagnostic teaching. The rate of improvement acts as an indicator of the type and severity of the handicap.

The causes of learning difficulties are seen as originating and reactive. Initially, both types may produce similiar behavioral symptoms.

The administrative advantages of a diagnostic-teaching procedure are that the psychologist works in partnership with the teacher, rather than as a tester. The procedure provides a realistic means, without testing, of selection for special education, and it makes possible systematic help for all children who have learning difficulties.

CHAPTER SIX describes a method of teaching designed to improve the child's learning skills. The child thereby becomes conditioned to learn that attention and reflectiveness bring success. Reinforcement is drawn from the opportunities for effectiveness that occur in children's play. Self-correcting gamelike activities provide a setting for natural learning that stands in contrast to teacher-monitored tasks and a teacher-centered curriculum.

The same principles of natural learning are applied in the remediation of difficulties in reading and mathematics, in which the stages have to be finely structured, with an understanding of the learning processes involved. Teachers need a better understanding of the phonic basis of reading.

Peer-monitored small-group activities enable remediation to begin in the regular classroom. If this fails, the child is withdrawn from the class part-time, and eventually for full-time special education if necessary. Primary teachers should be able to call on community volunteers; however, volunteers must be carefully organized.

CHAPTER SEVEN reviews the progress of 50 children treated in the Toronto Project. The remedial program served to differentiate between those children without intrinsic handicaps who quickly acquired good learning skills and those with ongoing handicaps of temperament or adverse circumstances who made slower progress. Diagnostic teaching of this type is a more realistic means of assessing the need for special education than is the use of standard tests.

CHAPTER EIGHT explores how permanent the gains of intervention will be. The biggest danger is that of throwing the child back into an unsuitable learning environment.

What constitutes a good learning environment should be worked out from our knowledge of the conditions under which learning in general takes place, and from practical, rather than formal, experiment.

Ten criteria for good conditions of learning are proposed as a means of assessing the learning environment and as a basis for teacher-training. These are:
1. Is the process of learning absorbing and rewarding?
2. Is there immediate knowledge of success or failure?

3. Is new learning based on existing capabilities?
4. Is each pupil able to work at his own level and pace?
5. Do pupils learn by their own mental activity?
6. Are there opportunities for peer-group learning?
7. Is time allowed for new knowledge to sink in?
8. Are the learning situations sufficiently varied?
9. Is the personal relationship between teacher and pupil conducive to learning?
10. Are physical conditions conducive to learning?

CHAPTER NINE discusses how the teacher's role can be objectified in order to ensure that every child enjoys good conditions for learning.

Rather than the teacher's developing a repertoire of styles to suit individual children, which is hardly practicable, the teacher should step off the center of the stage and become an organizer of the learning process.

Cases of 'misfit' between teacher and pupil should be thoroughly investigated as possible indications for diagnosis of inappropriate teaching methods or of maladjustment in the child. A typical case of 'misfit' is described in which both such diagnoses apply.

CHAPTER TEN gives detailed guidance to teachers in helping children overcome each of the 14 faulty learning approaches identified through the *Guide to the Child's Learning Skills,* and refers to the remedial materials designed for this purpose.

There are notes on the understanding and handling of the hostile child and the disruptive but creative child.

CHAPTER ELEVEN reports three studies of the extent to which the learning-to-learn effect of the Flying Start training is transferred to learning of different materials in different settings.

CHAPTER TWELVE lists the objections to medication as a standard therapy for the hyperactive child and proposes a diagnostic teaching approach as an alternative. Before instituting medication, the exact nature of the condition should be studied. "Try-it-and-see" diagnosis is unrealistic and clumsy.

The finding that what is learned under medication is not transferred to the natural state has serious implications, and underlines the need to develop alternative forms of treatment. Formal procedures are needed to prevent the indiscriminate use of drugs and to ensure that the causes of the hyperactivity are properly investigated and treated.

CHAPTER THIRTEEN restates the developmental alternative to 'intelligence' for the understanding of mental differences. Of the latter, individual variations in effectiveness-motivation are seen as important determinants that also directly affect learning in school.

Some suggestions are made about hitherto little-emphasized cultural influences on learning.

'Learning disabilities' as entities are seen as another stopgap type of explanation. They can be understood with fewer assumptions when learning failure is viewed behaviorally, taking into account the child's family setting and development.

Diagnosis should begin with a study of the way a child is failing to use his mental capabilities, followed by an exploration of his ability to respond to a program of conditioning in good learning and problem-solving strategies.

The study of learning failure should be extended to study of the ways we teach children. We need an explicit technology of teaching based on our understanding of the conditions for good learning.

APPENDIX A explains the method of use of the *Guide to the Child's Learning Skills*. A specimen and Profile Form are reproduced.

APPENDIX B gives the rationale of the Flying Start Learning-to-Learn materials as a means of correcting faulty learning habits. All of the items and their learning functions are described.

Introduction

The utilization of the psychologist as a helping professional in school systems had its inception in the early years of this century. The role of the school psychologist has been influenced and molded by a multiplicity of factors. Among the most important of these has been the relationship of psychology to medicine, the growth and development of special education services and programs, and the development and popularization of the standardized intelligence test.

Standardized intelligence tests were indeed developed in the first place for the purpose of determining quickly and efficiently which children could not be expected to cope with the curricula and methods of instruction in use. Although it was known from the beginning that such tests were not able to measure an individual's innate intellectual capacity, they were accepted outside the ranks of psychology as scientifically validated objective tools that would identify those incapable of learning. This misperception of the nature of the instruments, in addition to their administrative usefulness, made such instruments very attractive to school systems. School psychologists were usually hired by school systems in the first instance to administer, score, and interpret such tests of intelligence for the purpose of streaming children into special education programs. In the initial stages of the development of special education, such programs were usually designed for children who had been classified as being mentally retarded on the basis of intelligence test scores. Therefore, most school psychological services started out as psychometric departments that were not expected, and seldom allowed, to stray from their strictly psychometric function of classifying children intellectually.

Of course intelligence tests are not measures of innate intellectual capacity. They do not sample all intellectual functions, and ignorance of their nature can lead to the acceptance of self-fulfilling predictions. Because most such measures have been validated by school success and failure, they have been found to be good predictors of academic performance. Psychometric services were thus able to provide predictive data, assumed to be more objective than teachers' ratings, which would make it possible to siphon off "unintelligent" children into auxiliary programs where they would not suffer repeated failure and discouragement.

Despite its administrative popularity and practical simplicity, the mass use of standardized IQ tests in school systems can be seen, in retrospect, to have been a failure. The ease of administration of such instruments led to their wider and wider use, often by those ill-equipped for their interpretation. The lack of administrative influence suffered by school psychological services often increased the possibilities for misinterpretation and misuse. The central problem was, and is, that such tests tell us relatively little about *how* a child uses his intellectual capabilities, either ineffectively or not at all, or *why* he uses them. The testing movement typically gave short shrift to considerations of the extent to which children could be taught to use and develop their intellectual powers.

Because the psychometric model had so many serious limitations, a different mode of psychological service began to emerge in school systems. The role can best be characterized as that of a clinical psychologist, resident in a school system. This model of service usually went hand in hand with higher formal qualifications for the psychological practitioner. All this resulted in a more sophisticated form of service in which such instruments as standardized intelligence tests not only were utilized in a less simplistic manner, but also were increasingly regarded as only one device, among a plethora of instruments and techniques, that the clinician made use of in his professional practice

At the same time, the special education movement was gaining strength, and special education programs became not only more numerous but also more diverse and specialized. The clinical psychologist, therefore, was now required to assess children not only with respect to their suitability for slow-learner programs, but also with respect to their suitability for a wide range of special education services, including programs for the gifted, the emotionally disturbed, the learning disabled, etc.

A clinical model of school psychological service also has serious drawbacks. The most fundamental involves a consideration of the relationship of psychology to medicine. Because medicine in its own area has been so evidently successful, and because psychology as a fledgling profession has grown up under the shadow and, in many instances, the protection of medicine, psychology has often first taken root in medical settings. This has led to the practice of psychology being modeled, in many essential respects, on the practice of medicine. The problem that this poses for a school psychological service is simply that it tends to direct our attention to a single factor in the situation we are attempting to analyze. It tends to encourage the psychologist in the school system to focus on the child as the identified patient or client, and has tended to vitiate the psychologist's role in evaluating and influencing those other factors in the school situation that may be contributing, or even primary, factors in whatever the presenting problem happens to be. In other words, if the child is the identified patient, and the school psychologist's primary role is seen to be diagnosing what is wrong with the child and prescribing a course of action designed to ameliorate that condition, little more than lip service will be given to such vitally important considerations as the role of the teacher, the curriculum, etc. It has been comfortable for school systems to regard children experiencing learning failure as being in some sense "defective" or coming from "defective" homes. It has also been comfortable for school systems to employ psychologists as clinicians who will focus on the child's problems and on those of his parents.

Another major drawback to the clinical model of service is its inability to deal with the very large number of referrals usually generated. This dissatisfaction was heightened for us in Toronto by another consideration: We found that the bulk of our referrals consisted of children 8, 9, and 10 years of age. Such children had already experienced considerable frustration and failure in coping with the school system. This made it very much more difficult, and, in many cases, impossible, to mitigate, let alone reverse, the course of learning failure. We therefore determined to try to change our model of service. We wanted to become school psychologists rather than clinical psychologists resident in a school system. We wanted to address ourselves to all the factors that could be expected to have an important role in the learning process, rather than focusing primarily on the child and his parents. We wanted to make our services available to all children in the system, rather than to the relatively few with whom we were able to deal on a case by case basis. We wanted to make our service available to children early enough in their school careers that we might expect intervention to be effective with minimum expenditure of time and effort, so that fewer children would end up in special education programs.

To this end, in 1967 we instituted a mixed service and research program which we entitled "The Early Identification and Developmental Program." The research side of the program was an attempt to investigate a variety of instruments, techniques, and procedures for the early identification of children at risk educationally.[1]

The model of psychological service that resulted from that research endeavor has now become the primary mode of operation for our psychological service in Toronto. This has provided us with a means by which our staff may take the initiative in working in schools. Rather than relying on teacher referrals, our staff very largely do their own case finding. In the process they generate psychological data on all the children in a classroom, which is useful to the teacher in programming and curriculum development. The model also provides a method for providing very large numbers of children with varying degrees of psychological service, the degree of service being based on needs, which are determined by the psychological staff in conjunction with teachers and parents. Efficiency—the percentage of appropriate children receiving service—and effectiveness—the percentage of children receiving appropriate service—can, we believe, be very high under this method of operation, which provides for psychological involvement ranging from service to the whole classroom through service to small groups of students to more intensive service for individual children.

The identification aspect of this approach is a process, not an event. We have not attempted to develop or to construct a single instrument or single battery of techniques to be utilized in all situations. Our staff, in conjunction with their supervisors and the principal and teacher, use whatever procedures and instruments seem relevant to the age of the children, their background of experience, and the curriculum and behavioral expectations of the school. Thus, the specific instruments and techniques may vary from school to school, from year to year, and from psychologist to psychologist.

What is uniform is the procedure, which is essentially a succession of sieves of ever finer mesh. The first sieve consists of giving consideration to every child in the classroom. The second sieve involves a somewhat more extensive assessment of selected children, and the third sieve involves the kind of individual diagnostic assessment that used to be our first step when we worked under a referral system.

Identification is only a small part of the process, involving a minute fraction of the time commitment involved in a successful program. It

---

[1]Landrus, G. D., Brown, A. E., and Long, E. R. *The Toronto Early Identification and Developmental Program.* Toronto Board of Education, 1974.

should be stressed that, in this context, identification is not a labeling of children as suffering from quasi-diseases or as being necessarily bound for special education programs. Assessment is carried out in terms of the curriculum and behavioral expectations in the child's current class placement. It is expected that data will be generated that will help the teacher to program more effectively for all the children in her class and particularly for those who, for a wide variety of reasons, might be expected to run into difficulties unless some particular efforts are made.

Although we have used this model at virtually all age levels in our elementary and senior schools, our priority is to work with the children and teachers in kindergarten and Grades 1 and 2. The rationale for this is to attempt to maximize the effectiveness and efficiency of our work in an era of budget stringency and retrenchment. This form of psychological service obviously requires an extremely close and ongoing involvement of our staff with children, parents, and school personnel.

The aims of this model of school psychological service are two-fold. The first aim is to encourage the school psychologist to become engaged on a day-to-day basis with the whole process of education, rather than assuming a role as a somewhat alien 'expert' to whom problem children are referred. This concomitantly increases the responsibility of the school psychologist. For one thing, it engages him more intimately in the problem-solving task of finding more appropriate ways of teaching and dealing with children in a particular class in terms of all aspects of their developmental status. It also puts the responsibility for identifying children with serious problems on a shared basis, rather than primarily in the hands of the classroom teacher, as it is in the referral model.

The second main aim of this approach is to make it clear that the school psychologist has a number of constituencies, or clients. The most important of these, of course, is the child, but the parent is also the psychologist's client, as are the teacher and principal. In times past, it has seemed to some of us that school systems tended to regard only the principal and teacher as the legitimate clients of the psychological service.

There are obviously stresses and strains in instituting this type of service in a school system. In the short run, there is a hiatus during which the principal and teachers are faced with a large number of cases that they would like to refer to the psychological service. However, because of its commitment to a broader preventative approach, the service is otherwise engaged and is unable to provide an individual referral service at the level to which the school system had become accustomed. Understandably, it is also not always easy for teachers to allow the school psychologist the kind of partnership status and the assumption of an observational role in the classroom that such a program implies. Patience and tact are required on both sides. I would suggest too that the type and level of competence required by the school psychologist in such a system of service is of a high order, and is somewhat different from that which we have required from school psychological personnel in many jurisdictions in the past.

As I have described the outlines of our approach and the directions in which I see it developing, I have emphasized that the assessment procedures and their translation into data that can be of practical use to the teacher in the classroom have been left very largely in the hands of the local team, consisting of the teacher, principal, and our staff member. We felt that we would like to try this approach in a more highly structured and defined way in a small sample of schools.

We knew that Dr. Denis Stott, formerly of the University of Guelph, had developed a number of materials that seemed well-suited to this purpose. The materials could be used in a diagnostic or assessment capacity. They also include a number of systematic programs designed to supplement the curriculum in certain areas of assessed difficulty. We were fortunate in persuading Dr. Stott to join our staff on a part-time basis for the period of a school year so that he could demonstrate the use of his approach and his materials in six schools that volunteered for the project.

A. E. Brown, M.A., Ed.D.
Coordinator of Student Services
and Chief Psychologist,
Board of Education for the City of Toronto

The
Hard-to-Teach
Child

CHAPTER ONE

The
Toronto
Project

*If God were to offer me
the Truth in one hand
and the Search for Truth in the other,
I would choose the search.*
G. E. Lessing

This book grew out of a personal report submitted to the Student Services of the Toronto Board of Education on my work in the capacity of a part-time consultant to them during the fall and winter of 1975–1976. My only briefing was that Dr. A. E. Brown, Chief Psychologist to the Board, and his team of Senior Psychologists asked me to demonstrate in classrooms the approaches to learning difficulties that I had developed over the previous five or six years at the Center for Educational Disabilities at the University of Guelph.

Their invitation was symptomatic of a general disenchantment, present over the whole of the American continent, with a body of professional practice that hinged on the diagnosis of "deficits." Children have been, and still are, labeled according to particular deficits diagnosed by tests, and as a result of such assessment they are placed in the presumably appropriate type of special education. The role of the psychologist in this system has been primarily that of the tester—the diagnostician of the deficits. Such a procedure would be valid if the deficits diagnosed were disease entities for which methods of treatment of known effectiveness were available; however, as will be shown later by reference to recent research findings, this is by no means the case. The result has been a widespread concern about the dangers of mislabeling, especially in the case of socially disadvantaged children.

In recent years the Toronto Psychological Services and the Board's Research Department had made their contribution to the

1

movement for the early identification of educationally high-risk children, and their report had been published the previous year. In an ongoing study they showed that it was indeed possible to spot the great majority of such children. Their very success, however, raised the question of what measures might be taken to prevent the risk becoming actuality. The school psychological services foresaw that its role would increasingly be judged by its ability to contribute to remedial programs.

I should add to the above a tenet of my own personal philosophy that induced me to accept the briefing: I have always regarded it as the duty of a public system of education never to allow a child to vegetate in a condition of learning failure. How far off we are from realizing this ideal, even in the most advanced and financially well-supported boards, is objectively measured for us by the present rapid development of private agencies for the treatment of learning-disabled children. Their popularity is a mark of the failure of the public system to meet the legitimate demands of parents for effective remedial programs. It may of course be found that the child's handicap is irremediable, but at least parents should have sufficient confidence in the efforts of the public system on behalf of their child to feel assured that they will gain nothing by paying high fees in the private sector. Moreover, the fact that only a small minority of parents can afford such fees has the effect of sharpening the division between the advantaged and the disadvantaged. The acceptance of the principle that no child shall be allowed to remain unattended in a state of failure places upon us the same responsibility that the family doctor accepts for each of his patients. For the schools this responsibility means the frequent review of the progress of every child, especially in the early stages of education, and the calling-in of the appropriate specialist adviser the moment the teacher feels at the end of his resources. For the psychologist it means working intensively on a case until the child can cope within the regular class, or in turn securing whatever special educational treatment may be indicated.

My commitment to the Board consisted of one day a week, made up of one-half day a month in each of six elementary schools and the equivalent of one day a month with the team of psychoeducational consultants in whose areas the schools lay, and extended from the middle of September 1975 to the end of March 1976. The six schools were chosen to be representative of the variety of neighborhoods served by the Board. Because over half the student population of Toronto are recent immigrants, a large proportion, and in some cases the majority, of the children I worked with were New Canadians.

During my visits to the schools I was accompanied by Mr. Neville Fletcher, one of the Board's Senior Psychologists, and by the Psychoeducational Consultant for the area within which each school lay. Both stayed with me throughout my time in each school and shared my experiences. The latter maintained liaison with the teachers involved in the project during the intervening weeks in order to implement the remedial program.

I found my temporary colleagues torn between conflicting obligations. In the first place it was regarded as their duty to furnish the panel responsible for placing children in special classes with the result of standard tests. Second, they felt that it behooved them to apply the early identification procedure that they had helped to develop. Third, they had to deal with referrals of children from any grade within the elementary level, and if possible keep an eye on those already in special education. In no sense, therefore, did even the few who worked directly with me constitute a full-time project team.

A disadvantage of the assessment procedures used in the early identification program, and of nearly all the procedures developed in other quarters, was that it involved the testing of whole year-groups of young children. This consumed a great deal of time that might otherwise have been spent on the treatment of those considered likely to fail. Moreover, it could be asked whether or not the chief need is for formal procedures of identification. The teacher and the psychologist working together can probably pick out the educationally high-risk children. Feshbach, Adelman, and Fuller (1974) found that kindergarten teachers' ratings alone could predict first grade reading achievement at least as efficiently as a psychometric battery that had been designed for the purpose. Keogh and Smith (1970) also found that teachers were surprisingly accurate in early identification of both high-risk and high-potential children. Nevertheless, relying on the unguided judgment of individuals always introduces the personal variable: some teachers will always nominate more freely than others. Our strategy as psychologists might therefore be to systematize teachers' experience into standard methods of observation and reporting. This would reduce the time spent by the psychologists in identification to a small fraction of that taken up by the giving of tests.

A further barrier to full effectiveness lay in the traditional role of the psychologist as one who prescribes a course of treatment to the teacher. Such a form of communication presupposes the existence of well-established "prescriptions" like those a physician gives to a pharmacist. We cannot assume that the teacher has the necessary "bottles" on the shelf or that he would agree with the psychologist about how to use them if he did. Moreover, as an independent professional, a teacher is justified in using his judgment about the treatment of a particular child, including the choice of materials. Such a situation consequently demands the development of a close working liaison between two groups of professionals, and both will have to be convinced of the correctness of the diagnosis and the remediation.

The psychologist's contribution to this partnership is to make a diagnosis of the reasons for the poor performance, whether by tests or by observations of the child's functioning, and to translate this into recommendations based on what he knows as a psychologist about the learning processes, both cognitive and motivational. This part of his contribution cannot stop at generalities: the psychologist should be able to explain, and if need be, demonstrate, the procedures for arousing the learner's interest and inducing learning behavior. The teacher's part consists in appraising the recommendation and applying it, if approved in principle, to the child in question.

The above considerations defined my role, as I conceived it, in the project. I visited each school in the role of a school psychologist in order to advise teachers about children whom we jointly regarded as educationally high-risk. For administrative reasons it was decided that I should work in the Grade One classes. The half-day a month that I spent in each school was divided into two parts, so that I had the equivalent of a quarter day with each of the teachers, mostly in their own classrooms. In fact, one of the teachers withdrew because of poor health, but in another school a third teacher joined the project, so that I worked with twelve teachers as originally planned. Once the schools were chosen, the principals, in consultation with the area psychologist, chose those classes that contained a significant proportion of educationally high-risk children. Thus it was the classes, rather than the teachers, who were selected. Eight of them were regular Grade One, with a majority of children between six and seven years of age at the beginning of the school year; one class consisted of one-half such children and one-half children who were repeating Grade One; and three classes were primary special classes, in which the children were mostly a year or two older.

The project was never thought of as a formal experiment. Over the past generation we have gone through an agonizing struggle to establish educational findings by sophisticated research designs comparing matched groups. Samples were taken from broad categories of so-called retardates, slow learners, and learning-disabled, on the assumption that these represent homogeneous groups that would, in diverse neighborhoods and cultures, respond in the same predictable way to the experimental treatment. The procedures of matching with control groups were complicated by the fact that learning failure is the result of a tangled inter-action of factors. The attempt to eliminate or control for any one of them may deprive the researcher of a significant determinant; as Bannatyne (1975) puts it, we risk throwing out not one, but several, babies with the bathwater. The result of this research methodology has been a mass of nonsignificant or contradictory findings. Even if a significant result is obtained by the method of group comparison, it is likely to be uninformative. Guralnick (1973) points out that this result tells us neither which elements in the treatment chiefly produced the success nor with which kinds of children the treatment succeeded or failed, both of which are points of knowledge we need if we are going to advance and refine our procedures of treatment. Moreover, the group comparison method carries with it the presumption that the method of treat-ment to be used on the experimental group has already been perfected, or at least made as good as possible. In a formal experi-ment, once the procedure is chosen one is stuck with it; it must remain uniform, and its faults have to be faithfully repeated throughout the trials.

As far as I was concerned, I did not feel myself in a position to stipulate a set experimental procedure. Although the materials I had developed had been field-tested in regular kindergartens, one of which contained several recent immigrants, and in schools for the retarded, I had had no experience working in Grade One classes, and consequently knew little of the range of attainment to be expected. This applied particularly to the children recently ar-rived from other parts of the world. Quite a few of them came from the Caribbean, not only with little or no formal schooling but also with little idea of what was expected of them in a school setting. As far as those children who had been through kindergarten were concerned, I had to discover what training they had had in basic reading and number skills.

For these reasons I decided that I should not begin by holding training sessions with the teachers on how to use the learning materials, but rather by spending some time with each teacher in her classroom getting to know the educational level of her children and discussing her particular problems. I gave each child in the class a card and asked him to write his name and the numerals 1–10, then to draw a picture of himself, and of a dog and a cat, and to write the words "dog" and "cat" if he could. I attempted no analysis of the results of this impromptu test except for the writing of the numerals. Of the children in the regular Grade One classes, only 31% wrote the numerals from 1 to 10 correctly with no reversals; 17% had one numeral wrong, omitted, or reversed; 36% made two or more reversals; 12% could write only a few numerals or had no idea of their order; and 4% could not, or did not, write any numerals. It is of interest, in view of the diagnostic importance sometimes attached to reversals, that the great majority of these Grade One children reversed at least one of their numerals.

CHAPTER TWO

Recent Developments in The Field of Learning Problems

*No science has ever been
entirely composed of some neat collection of truths
in which scientists, a body of men set apart by their knowledge,
all concur.*
C. C. Gillespie

The project described in this report is typical of a major reorientation in thinking about learning problems that is taking place throughout the American continent. A perusal of the recent literature within the fields of learning disabilities and mental retardation reveals an ongoing questioning of an erstwhile confidently held theory and of the practices that stem from it. This theory and practice centered on a belief in the biological inevitability of a range of deficits that acted as handicaps to learning.

Of these hypothesized deficits the foremost relates to an undefinable quality of mind conceived of as intelligence as measured by the IQ. Kamin (1974) has dug into psychological history to reveal the ill-uses to which mental testing has been put, especially in discrimination against ethnic minorities. In so far as poor test performances of ethnic minority children are still taken at face value, the abuse and injustice continues. Lloyd Dunn (1968) has characterized traditional intelligence testing as "digging the

7

educational graves of many racially and/or economically disadvantaged children." As a criterion for placement in special schools for the educable and trainable retarded, intelligence testing resulted in filling them with a disproportionate number of Black children. Jones (1972) quotes the finding of the California State Department of Education that, whereas non-Whites comprised only 21% of enrollment in the state's public schools, they occupied 52% of the places in classes for the mildly retarded.

Ideas that everyone cherishes are accepted uncritically, and their contradictions overlooked. There has been curiously little research on the validity of the idea that each individual is born with a certain amount of basic intelligence that remains constant throughout life and in every situation. This writer (Stott, 1960, 1961) examined the changes in Terman-Merrill IQs of 952 English children in special schools for the educationally subnormal who had been tested two or more times, giving 1358 test-retest comparisons. I found that 28% of them changed 10 points or more, and, among these, 11% changed 15 points and 3.5% 20 points or more. A small number showed gains or losses of 30–33 points. The known poor standardization of the Terman-Merrill for subnormal children could not account for the IQ changes: the net mean fall on retest (after intervals of up to five years) was only 2.2 points, whereas the net change was 7.1 points, one third of which were gains. Nor was it a matter of different testers: the net change with the same tester was 6.8, compared with 7.5 with a different tester, but even this discrepancy disappeared when the interval was greater than two years. A telltale indication was that it was mostly the boys who were the gainers, the net mean fall being two and one-half times greater for the girls. This suggests that there was some genuine developmental factor behind the IQ changes. A critical piece of research, which to this writer's knowledge has never been carried out, would be a study of the reasons for large IQ gains or losses in individual children. It might be as revealing as the study by Walker (1975) on the reasons for hyperactivity, which is referred to below.

No doubt it was the growing disillusionment with the IQ that induced Garrison and Hammill (1971) to examine the inconsistency of performance of educable mentally retarded children in various test items. Having established criteria for intellectual normalcy from 319 control children, they found that 25% of the 378

EMR (mildly mentally retarded) children passed four out of five of the criteria.

> While some of these children scored minimal passes on each criterion... other children evidenced impressive scores on the criteria and could in no way be considered 'retarded' or 'dull'... numerous students made inexplicably high marks on several criteria while failing the others. These curiously high scores suggested that on at least two intellectual tasks, and possibly more, the child was capable of successful performance.

Baumeister and Muma (1975) extend these doubts to the definition of mental retardation put forward by the American Association for Mental Deficiency, on the grounds that it rests upon the concept of a homogeneous level of intelligence. In their opinion, the IQ, as a complex outcome of a large number of influences, "cannot, or at least should not, be used to 'diagnose' anything." In particular they point to the absurdity of using arbitrary cut-off scores, such as 50 or 70, as criteria for placement in different types of special education. They advocate the abolition of a unitary conception of mental retardation in favor of continuous observation of how the retarded person copes and progresses.

As intelligence tests came into general use it was found that "low intelligence" did not by any means account for all cases of learning failure; many children, especially middle- and upper-class boys, were unable to learn despite having average or even superior IQs. Instead of questioning the concept of an all-pervasive level of mental ability, psychologists and special-educators explained these anomalies by a post hoc supplement to the ability/deficit theory, which in science is recognized as a mark of theoretical weakness. It was hypothesized that a large discrepancy between a child's IQ and his academic achievement must be attributable to some deficit other than that of intelligence. This became, in effect, the diagnostic touchstone for the existence of a "learning disability" (Bateman, 1965; Myklebust and Johnson, 1967).

The language used—"having a learning disability," "having dyslexia," etc.—elevated these hypothetical constructs to the status of disease entities. Like the notion of intelligence, they became self-sufficient explanations that prevented people from looking further. The tendency of many "learning-disabled" children to reverse letters and numerals and to copy shapes inaccurately was attributed to anomalies of perception. It was comforting to their parents to learn that their children were not mentally subnormal but merely saw the world the wrong way round, and so the notion of perceptual handicap became popular and was rapidly assimilated into the mythology of our culture. It was overlooked that during his first weeks of life the young child has to learn to recognize objects irrespective of which way round they are. If he failed to do this he would have to learn to recognize every object afresh each time he saw it from a different angle. At the early stages of a child's perceptual development, direction not only may be, but also has to be, ignored. Only when a child encounters graphic symbols does direction become critical: to learn that a letter means something different according to the way it faces requires a special effort to counteract the earlier generalization that direction does not matter, which is still valid as far as the recognition of everyday things is concerned. Pavlov has shown that it is very difficult to erase firmly established learning; unless the new, corrective learning is constantly reinforced the old reasserts itself. I mentioned earlier that the great majority of the 6- to 7-year-old Toronto children in *regular* classes in which I worked had not yet completely mastered this special directional learning in the writing of numerals. It is evidently normal for young children to reverse letters and numerals at the beginning of the educational process. Consequently we have to ask why some children continue to show directional confusions. The first possibility to explore, since it is a matter of learning, is that these children may have generally poor learning skills, or for some educational or social reason have not been able to carry out the special learning needed to counteract the earlier learning. Later it will be argued that the critical variable in learning is that of the use or non-use, in other words, of the occurrence or non-occurrence, of cognitive processes. If a child, as a result of the impulsivity of his temperament or lack of training, does not attend to or process information, learning will not occur. Such lack of learning skill is typical of the classic hyperactive child. It is thus no coincidence that the hyperactive child, so termed, tends to show directional confusions. It is more plausible to attribute these to his observed poor skills of attention and reflection than to some cerebral anomaly for which there is no independent evidence. The same principle applies to the culturally disadvantaged. Deutsch (1963) found that impoverished children have inferior auditory and visual discriminations, but no physical sensory defects to account for such. Summarizing Deutsch's findings, Grotberg (1970) concluded that "A nondeveloping nervous system may indeed produce the same learning disability symptoms as a damaged learning system."

Other specific learning disabilities can similarly be explained from what we know about cognitive processes, without our having to postulate unverifiable anomalies. Sometimes children are said to have a defect of short-term memory: the teacher complains that the child forgets a word a moment after he has been told it, or he writes a word correctly on one line and hopelessly incorrectly on the next. The first thing I look for in such cases is evidence of the child's having been subjected to such intense pressures, or of the learning process having become so acutely painful to him that he cannot bear to keep his mind on the learning task. This is a matter of mental blockage caused by an avoidance process that is beyond his conscious control. Then we have "short attention span." Broman (1970) studied a series of children in whom this supposed deficit had been diagnosed, and found that they concentrated well when they were active and creative on their own initiative. The short attention span was related to a lack of interest in the subject matter. Broman concluded that "A short attention span is a symptom, not a cause"—one might say a symptom more of our failure to motivate children rather than of their intrinsic inability to attend.

The inability of a child to reproduce the figures of the Bender-Gestalt Test may often seem difficult to interpret except in terms of disturbance of perception attributable to minimal brain dysfunction. Although it may be such, in my experience it is very rarely so. To distinguish between a triangle and a square entails first having developed triangle and square concepts. If the individual has little use for such concepts he is unlikely to make these discriminations. Many travellers have remarked how clumsy tribal Africans were in handling rectangular boxes: their containers and huts were round. In our own culture, disadvantaged children sometimes lump together all geometrical figures as "shapes." Similarly, the impulsive, hyperactive child has never learned to "use his eyes" and has probably never attended to geometrical patterns, just as we have never attended to the reading of footprints. Moreover, he has probably lacked the patience to translate a shape into motor behavior. His perceptual handicap is more likely to be a lack of perceptual experiences and non-occurrence of cognitive processes than a structural deficit.

Rather than jump to the conclusion that learning disabilities imply cerebral anomaly or dysfunction, we should make studies of how conceptual anomalies and deficits may occur. An unexpected finding by a British Infants Head teacher[1] is thought-provoking in this connection. She interviewed the parents of all the children in her school who were having learning difficulties in order to gain insight into the reasons. Many of the parents reported that their children spent all their leisure hours watching TV. The principal found that these children were notably unable to interpret static pictures, to focus on any feature of a picture, or to attend to a particular word in a sentence. Apparently the type of perceptual scanning required for getting meaning from a moving picture is quite different from that required for the interpretation of the detail of a static image. These children had apparently handicapped themselves perceptually by their concentration upon TV presentations, and consequently they lacked the types of attentional skills needed for school learning. Such a finding needs experimental verification, but even as a plausible hypothesis it should make us cautious about attributing learning deficits to an organic anomaly.

In the United States an imposing edifice of professional qualification and practice has been erected upon the concept of learning disabilities as structural deficits. It has not stood the test of formal research. Larsen and Hammill (1975) reviewed 60 studies that correlated attainment in reading and arithmetic with the four most recognized perceptual deficits, i.e., visual discrimination, spatial relations, visual memory, and auditory-visual integration. They found that none of them produced correlations as high as 0.35, which they took as indicating a significant relationship. They concluded that "measured visual-perceptual skills are not sufficiently related to academic achievement to be particularly useful."

The same authors (Hammill and Larsen, 1974) show that the results of training children in psycholinguistic skills, reviewed over 38 studies, were inconclusive. Buckland and Balow (1973) found that low-readiness Grade One children trained over two months with the Frostig worksheets showed no significant gains in perceptual skills, readiness, or word-recognition skills compared with children who listened to stories.

Such small improvements as have been obtained by perceptual training programs have tended to be with boys. This again suggests that the deficit was not so much in perceptual ability as in attention

---

[1]Mrs. Dorothy Higgs, Moseley Infant's School, Coventry.

(Halliwell and Solan, 1972). Samuels and Turnure (1974) found that when boys can be made to attend as well as girls the sex difference favoring the latter disappears.

In summary, it looks as if disability-producing deficits have become an academic myth—a myth that is convenient to the college academic and school psychologist because it provides an apparently authoritative and final explanation, convenient to parents because it absolves them from the shame of having a dull or retarded child, and convenient to the teacher because it excuses what looked like teaching failure. It is understandable that, if the machinery is available for doing so, a frustrated teacher who can make no headway with a child is tempted to ask for him to be tested on suspicion of mental retardation or perceptual handicap, with a view of his being removed to another educational setting. It is easy to understand the concern of Pat Lane, Editor of the *Journal of Learning Disabilities*, lest her field of special education "become the 'dumping ground' for kids who couldn't make it in the mainstream of education."

Loss of confidence about the learning-disability/deficit concept is even spreading to those specialist teachers whose training has been in this field. "The LD teachers," writes Grossman (1975), "report that they and their colleagues are frequently plagued with considerable doubts about the meaning, or even the validity, of their professional activities."

The frustration of the LD specialist teacher is turned upon the makers of the labels. One such teacher is quoted by Grossman as saying, "The trouble with these psychologists is that all they've ever done is test kids. They've never sat down in a classroom with them and seen what they're like. . . . It is as if the psychologist accepts only the responsibility to forward the student on." Other teachers complained that the assessment "contained few, if any clues towards prescribing a course of classroom strategies."

It is unfortunate that the altogether praiseworthy aim of identifying educationally high-risk children at as early an age as possible was seen in terms of the deficit mystique. Kindergarten and Grade One children have been subjected to hours of testing, the predictive value of which may be no better than their teacher's observations. In a clear-sighted article, Koegh and Becker (1973) put this search for future learning deficits in young children in a common-sense perspective. They regard as justified the identification of handicapping conditions *that already exist*. However, attempts to spot failure before it occurs is "hypothesizing rather than confirming"—and doing so at a low predictive level. They foresee that

> Emphasis in early identification may well be changed from a future orientation to one that is more concerned with what is needed for success in the present or immediate future. The closer the measure and criterion are in content and time, the more likely that the prediction is, in fact, identification.

They advocate "direct observation of classroom behavior and analysis of children's problem-solving styles," not only as probably the most effective means of identification, but also as providing a realistic basis for remediation.

Up to this point my argument must appear more as a demolition job than as a constructive new approach. Left as it stands, it could lead to a lack of confidence in educational psychology and leave a theoretical vacuum in special education. It is not hard to foresee that, if an alternative theory and technology are not forthcoming to fill this vacuum, budget-conscious school boards might begin to think of dispensing with psychologists and special-education services. The need for working guidelines has been well summed up by Vera Reilly (1970), past President of the Council for Educational Diagnosis and Programming:

> (Teachers) want practical information from a behavioral point of view. In other words, they want to know exactly how to teach the child. In the past, they have not gotten this information. The child has been categorized with a psychomedical label by his performance on a standarized test and placed in a class on this basis. This tells the teacher nothing about the kind of learning environment the child needs, what motivates him, his particular academic and social strengths and weaknesses, or how to program for them.

This is the challenge that school psychologists have to meet, and in the chapter of this book on remediation I put forward some proposals about how we might do so. However, we must fill the theoretical vacuum. In the following two chapters I discuss how this may be done. The first suggests a way of accounting for differences in mental development and performance other than by level of intelligence. The second aims to fill what has always been an awkward gap in our theories of learning: how we get the child to want to learn and to enjoy learning.

CHAPTER THREE

Mental
Capability

Once preconceived ideas are cleared away,
the rest is simple.
Arthur C. Clarke

As early as 1925, H. A. Overstreet, then Professor of Philosophy at
New York City College, wrote:

> The mind is no mystical entity, existing in aloof, metaphysical
> changelessness as either commonplace or distinguished. *The mind is
> what it does.* Or better still, *the mind becomes what it does.* Give a mind
> something new to feed upon, give it something new to do, and it
> becomes a different mind. [Overstreet's italics.]

In the heyday of mental testing, "intelligence" was regarded as
just such a mystical entity of metaphysical changelessness, and
Overstreet's highly unfashionable view was conveniently ignored.
For a whole generation hardly a voice was heard in protest against
the notion of a measurable "intelligence," of which every person
was assumed to be endowed with a fixed quantity. It was claimed
that a mental tester was able to tap the child's innate mental capacity by means of a test with only a small margin of error. The notion
was biologically preposterous. A brain with a fully developed capacity available at any one time, without regard for previous use or
training, would be unique among organs. No one supposes that
every individual carries a musculature fully developed and available to capacity.

It was probably the publication of *Intelligence and Experience* by
J. McV. Hunt (1962) that opened the way for an explanation of
intellectual growth that accorded both with biological feasibility
and common sense. Hunt rejected the notion of intelligence as a
constant essence, and conceived of it as representing mental skills
that a child accumulates from interacting with his environment.
He came to regard intelligence tests merely as samplings of behavior—and the statistically derived factors of the intellect that

15

have dominated psychometry for a generation as probably having no relation to the true structure of the mind or how it works. Gagné's (1968) theory of cumulative intellectual growth traced the development of the child's capabilities from the point where he first notes associations and begins to recognize similarities and to make distinctions. From the regularities he observes, the child develops generalized expectancies in the form of concepts and rules. Simple rules—or as we might say, simple understanding—lead to more complex rules and understanding. "The child . . . learns an ordered set of capabilities which build on each other in progressive fashion." In short, each thought is the product of every thought that has gone before it. Each solution achieved is an event in a life-long programming in problem-solving skills. If a child has not been through the requisite mental programming he is unprepared for the demands we make upon him in school and in tests. He would be like a typical American trying to understand a cricket match, or a Briton trying to follow baseball. No psychometric magic can bridge the developmental gap.

Moreover, success in solving one problem makes the child more willing to attempt further problems of a similar kind, and as he proceeds to solve these also he becomes conditioned to expect success in other problem-solving activities. In such circumstances his self-programming will proceed apace. If, on the other hand, he meets a problem for which he is unprepared, he will become bewildered and discouraged. No further problems of that kind will be attempted, and his mental development is by so much brought to a halt. In the one case the child's mind is being well used, and in the other case poorly used and developed. The endstate, as assessed by an IQ test, may be attributable as much as to the degree of use of the mind as to a hypothetical quality or ability. The recorded score makes no distinction, and we are never justified in assuming inability rather than non-use.

This theory enables us to understand not only the growth but also the lack of growth of intellect. Bruner (1968) has compared the development of mental capabilities to that of a technology. No single brain can make the requisite advances; they have to be assimilated from the culture. Children have to be taught to think by a human environment that provides models for ordering experience and strategies for solving problems. Ausubel (1969) points out that an environment that deprives the child of these techniques for understanding and thinking about his world produces cumulative handicap. If the earlier steps have been missed the child cannot profit from subsequent experiences, and the retardation becomes permanent.

These developmental theories of mental growth and differences lend feasibility to Overstreet's bold statement that the mind, given new experiences and new scope for use, becomes a different mind. In other words, the changes are qualitative. As Gordon (1973) has put it:

> Use creates a new organization, a new structure, which is then put to use in a movement toward more and more complex structures. . . . Provision of early experience enhances development; lack of experience retards it. It may be that such retardation is temporary in humans, and can be overcome by later experience; but, as in sports, the game of 'catch-up' is far harder to win than the game of staying ahead.

Gordon goes on to ask, "How competent can man become?" He draws the logical deduction that the limits are very open. There is no justification for our arbitarily fixing them for any individual by the result of a test: "Our present measurements of intelligence, achievement, or abilities may be operating in a feedback way to deter us from recognizing the potential in ourselves and our children." The practical conclusion that Gordon draws is that "We need to stop using our tests as gateposts for the denial of experience and as criteria for admission to experience, because in so doing we limit the possibilities for an individual to stretch himself."

That the view of a fixed intelligence can have this restrictive influence is forcibly put forward by Feuerstein (1968) in the field of mental retardation. He has named it the passive acceptant approach, which "reflects the more or less overt assumption that the retarded individual is essentially unmodifiable . . ." he continues that ". . . tests themselves are accomplices to the perpetuation of retarded performance levels" since they do not measure "the hidden capacity of the individual to function differently given proper conditions."

As a way of understanding the varying mental capabilities of individuals, this developmental, open-ended concept is so much in accordance with what we know about other aspects of human development that we have to ask why, with the support of so many leading authorities, it has not banished the opposing view of everyone's having a given "intelligence." The reason would appear to be that this latter notion has become embedded in the thinking of our culture as an explanatory factor that has a seductive surface plausibility. When we observe individuals functioning mentally at different levels it is hard not to see this as evidence of different "levels of intelligence." In terms of the theory summarized above, an individual's mental development as it is at any one time would be treated as a result, not a cause. To infer an entity or structure called intelligence as a causal factor puts us back to the level of prescientific thinking. Referring to the cognate concept of instincts, Endler and his co-authors (1968) write: "This approach is almost certainly an explanatory cul-de-sac, unless at the same time the instinct and its way of influencing the organism are quite clearly defined (and related to observable phenomena)." The notion of intelligence is likewise an explanatory cul-de-sac that leads us no further than the proposition that intelligence is intelligence is intelligence. It is a comfortable bedrock explanation at which all further inquiry and understanding stops. Those who require some verbal peg upon which to hang the developmental explanations of individual differences in mental growth might consider substituting the term 'capabilities' for that of 'intelligence'; it contains the ideas of skill and competence, which are connected with learning and doing, and so are unlikely to be reified into a "constant essence."

Naturally, in our quest for the causes of poor mental development and functioning we shall have to take account not only of brain damage and dysfunctions of a physiological nature but also of congenital, including genetic factors, but any such will have to be specific and demonstrable. No self-respecting geneticist would accept a behavioral-developmental conglomerate such as the IQ as a phenotype from which a pattern of inheritance could be induced, and Kamin's contention (1974), based on a well-documented scrutiny of the classical twin and sibship studies, that there is so far no evidence for the heritability of the IQ, must be accepted until someone can refute his critique. He shows that the work of even the greatest protagonists of heritability, such as Burt, was ill-reported to the length of cover-up, and was methodologically slovenly and biased.

It is an unfortunate truism of research that studies that everyone is inclined to accept are seldom critically scrutinized. Notably, the psychometricians, who needed the concept of a general intelligence as the theoretical underpinning of their test-making, could afford to be careless about the concept because virtually everyone in the academic world believed in it. For example, Jensen

(1969), in his well-known monograph, avoided the issue by declaring, "There is no point in arguing the question to which there is no answer, the question of what intelligence really is" (pp. 5–6). Within a few pages he provides us with contradictory answers: on page 8, "intelligence, by definition, is what intelligence tests measure," yet eleven pages later it is "a biological reality," and represents "an aspect of objective reality, just as much as do atoms, genes, and electromagnetic fields." The falsity of the scientific analogy lies in the lack of evidence for a specific structure that we may call intelligence. We only have evidence of differences, admittedly vast, in the performance of individuals on certain mental tasks that we have traditionally considered as marks of "intelligence" in our culture.

Nor does it give the IQ more plausibility to fall back on its correlation with academic success. The same advantages and disadvantages that determine academic success could also feasibly make for success on an intelligence test—the background of everyday knowledge, training in habits of attention, discrimination and reflectivity, familiarity with print and with the pencil-and-paper techniques of education, and the incidental but massive acquisition of concepts from daily experiences in the life of an educated family. In contrast to these are the cumulative early discouragement and turning off with which the disadvantaged understandably react to their bewilderment and failure, not to mention the more material variables of nutrition, health care, living space, quiet and sleep, and exposure to day-to-day stresses and calamities.

If a low IQ test score tells us anything, it is that in certain fields of mental function the child is performing poorly. Once we have learned to resist the temptation to attribute this to "low intelligence," a low IQ score or any other indication of poor performance can become the starting point for an inquiry into its cause. As Budoff (1974) puts it, the low IQ score is a danger signal that the child needs help.

Once freed from the concept of "intelligence" as an all-too-easy explanation, we can look beyond the poor mental performance to discover its cause. Walker's (1975) approach to hyperactivity affords us an excellent methodological model. He refused to be content with a form of diagnosis that consisted of merely attaching a label. He regarded the observed hyperactive behavior as "a constellation of signs and symptoms that can occur for various reasons." Realizing that it usually indicated some sort of brain dysfunction, he proceeded to search for forms of physiological mal-functioning that could affect the brain. Because oxygen supply is the most critical element in normal brain function, he looked for pathological conditions that could interfere with it, and he found instances of heart anomaly, the correction of which cured the hyperactivity. In other cases he found the brain dysfunction to be attributable to incipient diabetes, calcium deficiency, glandular dysfunction, or lead or carbon monoxide poisoning. Sometimes the hyperactivity was attributable to purely incidental reasons, such as the discomfort of tight clothing. (I have known a case of a young child's using excessive activity to distract his mind from a chronic pain to which he could not give expression.)

Walker pointed out that if he had merely made a diagnosis of hyperactivity, and applied the usual drug treatment, the above conditions would have remained undetected. A whole new world of diagnostic possibilities await us if, in the same way, we look upon the symptoms of poor mental development and functioning as the results of a number of possible causes that need to be investigated.

CHAPTER FOUR

The Motivation
of
Learning

If the motivation is powerful enough,
the most clever among us can become fools,
and often the most stupid clever.
La Rochefoucauld

In our search for a theory of motivation we have to ask ourselves what we can appeal to in the child in order to induce him to organize his experiences into concepts and to think out and to try solutions—in other words, to embark upon the process that Overstreet and Gordon regard as the key to good mental development. Very little attention has been given to this aspect of education.

Also thinking in terms of maximizing capability, Budoff (1974) demands that we "seek instructional formats that *engage* the child and allow him to enhance his sense of continuing competence." Particularly for the disadvantaged, he argues, we need "to provide successes which will be competence-enhancing for the child and reverse his early expectation of failure." I was particularly pleased to note Budoff's emphasis of the need to enhance the child's sense of his own competence. By observation of my own children many years ago, I was able to make a classification of the types of goals that are reinforcing to children in their play, and showed that these could be summed up in a generalized need to interact effectively with their world. At about the same time that I published this study (Stott, 1961), White (1959) made a similar analysis of the play of Piaget's children and induced a need for competence. I have come to regard this need for effectiveness or competence—universally present, albeit in varying degrees, in all but the vegetable-like idiot—as an important motivation in learning. In the first place it generates curiosity, the need to know about one's environment as a condition for manipulating it. Second, it includes recognition,

21

which involves a generalization of similar features in objects and thence leads to the formation of concepts. To deal effectively with his environment a child has to note differences. Pleasure in discrimination is thus an aspect of effectiveness-motivation. The more a child is able to organize his experiences into concepts, the greater will be his success over an ever-widening range of operations. And so we find an innate pleasure in reflectivity as a further aspect of this motivation. However, the need for effectiveness or competence does not stop at the stages of input and mental organization. It demands the use of knowledge to bring about changes in one's world. The individual envisions a change that he judges to be within his powers, and sets himself the goal of achieving it. In a young child it may be merely filling a can with pebbles, or fitting things together, or breaking something into pieces—anything, so long as some spectacular effect is produced, some goal realized, some pattern or regularity discerned, or some information or understanding gained. In this way the motivation towards a progressively greater effectiveness contributes still further to mental development. When a piece of knowledge is tested by being used, it is incorporated into the permanent register of fully mastered, serviceable knowledge and contributes to the individual's general capability.

The need for effectiveness may indeed be the main variable determining levels of mental development. A child needs such a feeling in order to overcome his own fears: fear of what is strange and novel, fear of being unable to cope with a situation, or fear of the risks involved in experimenting and learning. Consequently we find that children poorly endowed with the urge to effectiveness may shrink from all new experience and cannot be persuaded to try anything that looks difficult. The most extreme cases of this handicap of temperament form a class of mental retardates, cases of which will be found in any school for the subnormal. We can have no idea what their mental capabilities might otherwise have been, because they have never developed their minds. All we can say, from observations of their poor concept formation and their poor performance, is that their mental development is retarded.

It is curious that children with very high effectiveness-needs can also experience learning difficulties. They do not agree to do what the teacher wants them to do or in the way that the teacher wants. They insist on adding something of their own, which at best may be creative or imaginative, but which is more often seen as sidetracking the issue and being disruptive. A not insignificant proportion of the young children referred to our Guelph Center were of this type. Because of their high level of activity they were pronounced hyperactive, but they did not at all conform to the classical concept of the hyperactive child, with an attention-focusing difficulty and poor perceptual capabilities.

The child Ryan, described by Dr. Marie O'Neill in Chapter Eleven, is a case in point. His habit of running around the classroom over the table tops could be regarded as the epitome of hyperactivity, but climbing on to some elevated object and walking on something high are elemental forms of expression of effectiveness-motivation commonly observed not only in humans but also in animals. Young animals as well as children play forms of the game "I'm King of the castle!" Unlike the perceptually inept hyperactive child, Ryan showed great skill at the Flying Start puzzles. He put them together without error, and worked so quickly that it was impossible to check his work before he was away again, rushing around the room to look at the other children's efforts. Again, in contrast to our traditional conception of hyperactivity, when doing the Raven Matrices test he listened to instructions and pondered his responses. On the Marble Sorter test of effectiveness-motivation (Stott and Albin, 1975) he attempted to shake the marbles into their seatings, a self-imposed task that implied good powers of observation, and incidentally gave him a near-maximum score. Ryan operated according to his own ideas, but at a high level of effectiveness. He made his presence felt in spectacular ways, showed an interest in everything, and lost no opportunity to exercise competence. In short, he crammed an enormous output of effectiveness into every minute of his day. His behavior certainly was disruptive and alarming, because it did not in the least conform to the kind of discipline a teacher needs in order to develop the capabilities of young children. He could certainly run into serious trouble if no one took him in hand and directed his high effectiveness-needs into productive channels.

A great deal more research is needed in effectiveness-motivation, especially with regard to its deficiency as a source of mental retardation and its excess as a source of learning failure and deviance. At least in young children, it is a variable that can be measured (Stott and Sharp, 1976) and shows consistency in a variety of situations (Stott, Williams, and Sharp, 1976). Hutt and Bhavnani (1972) have shown that qualities of explorativeness and inventiveness in children, which are aspects of effectiveness-motivation, show a considerable constancy over four or five years.

It is proverbial that every advance in knowledge opens up fresh issues. Having identified children's varying effectiveness-needs as an important component in mental development, we are led to ask why these needs vary so much. There is some evidence that pregnancy stresses play a part (Stott, 1959a), which is consistent also with more general findings in this area (Stott, 1973a; Stott and Latchford, 1976). However, the effects of such stresses have been shown, through experimental studies with animals, to be dependent on the genotype of the mother and child. Apart from this, I consider that there are general theoretical reasons for a genetic factor in effectiveness-needs, and, in so far as any such factor is established in mental development, it could be through variations in this motivational mechanism rather than through some unidentified quality of the cognitive processes themselves.

CHAPTER FIVE

Assessment

The continuous invention
of new ways of observing
is man's special secret of living.
J. Z. Young

The abandonment of the notion that every person is endowed with a more or less fixed level of intelligence that can be measured and expressed in an IQ has reduced mental testing to an anachronism. Moreover, it is becoming widely recognized that standardized mental tests tell us little about the way in which the child is functioning in the classroom (Novack et al., 1973; Neisworth and Greer, 1975). In addition, there is the danger, first, of assumptions about low intelligence creating discrimination against children who have not had the opportunity to develop the concepts regarded as normal in our culture; and, second, of discouraging the teachers from making an effort to develop latent capabilities in the child.

Some of us may rationalize our continued use of mental tests as at least measuring the contemporary state of the child's functioning. This would be justified if the result were expressed in some form other than a quotient, which takes for granted a frequency distribution of level of intelligence, and if we could be assured that the results of the testing were not interpreted by other people as representing the *limits* of a child's functioning. Unfortunately, in a culture steeped in the professional myth of intelligence as a measureable quantity, we cannot have this assurance. It is far more likely, as Budoff put it, that a low IQ will be used "to reify the child's failure to learn into a mandate to expect little and an excuse to challenge the child little."

An implication of the developmental approach for assessment is that the extent to which mental powers are used is responsible for greater differences in performance than any hypothetical variable of intrinsic quality. The fact of the occurrence or non-occurrence of a thought *must* be more important than its precise quality, if and when it does occur. If this sounds like a heresy I can only plead that I am in good company. From their work with monkeys and sub-

25

sequently with young children, Harlow and Harlow (1949) concluded that "Thinking does not develop spontaneously as an expression of innate abilities; it is the end result of a long learning
process." "What is significant about the growth of the mind in the
child," writes Bruner (1968), "is to what degree it depends not
upon capacity but upon the unlocking of capacity by techniques
that come from exposure to the specialized environment of a culture." Probably the most important training conferred upon the
child by an advanced culture is in the techniques of learning itself.
A used mind becomes a developed mind, and an unused one remains undeveloped.

It follows that the main target of assessment should be the
study of this use, poor use, and non-use. Such information is of
direct relevance to remedial programming: it shows us, in behavioral terms, why the child is failing—what Margaret Vernon
(1957) called the "events of failure." Behind such poor use or
non-use there may lie further handicaps in the form of cognitive or
motivational deficits, but these can be revealed only when every
opportunity has been given to the child to bring his mind to bear
upon learning tasks.

What is really important to assess, in short, is the extent to
which we can teach the child to use and develop his mental powers.
There is absolutely no way of doing this except by working with the
child in a remedial program and observing the degree to which his
capacity for learning can be developed. As Dunn puts it, "the instructional program itself becomes the diagnostic device."
Haywood (1976) calls for

> assessment techniques that lead to development-enhancing proce-
> dures in a direct way rather than to static classification ... the pro-
> cesses of assessment and of intervention are intertwined deliberately,
> so that some intervention takes place during assessment, and assess-
> ment continues throughout the process of intervention.

During the 1960s research workers in different parts of the
world were independently arriving at a similar new conception of
assessment. In Massachusetts, Budoff developed his system of
learning potential measurement. Having observed how many children could improve by practice on a mental test, he argued that we
should cease to regard this merely as a contamination of the result,
but as a significant psychological dimension that is not tapped by
the traditional measures. His procedure aims to assess the child's
ability to learn and to profit from experiences. He used traditional

test material for such assessment, but envisaged a whole new type of educational process based on the enhancement of the child's sense of his own competence.

In Israel, Feuerstein has developed his Learning Potential Assessment Device (Feuerstein, 1978) for use with the retarded, the aim of which "is to assess general learning modifiability, the amount of teaching investment necessary to bring about changes." To this end he formulates an explicit strategy, which he calls mediated learning experience. Essentially it consists of providing the child with carefully selected and ordered experiences, teaching him to capitalize upon them and to use them for further problem-solving. His methodology stands in sharp contrast to the all-too-fashionable practice of merely immersing the child in unorganized, chance experiences without providing him with the mental techniques to profit by them.

The work in progress in England at the National Foundation for Educational Research under Dr. Hegarty may be quoted as a further example of how, once minds are liberated from a dominant concept, workers in different parts of the world arrive independently at the new approach. This work originated in efforts to assess young immigrant children. To quote from the brief outline:

> The underlying rationale is based on the notion of learning ability rather than intelligence. The aim is to assess the child's ability to respond to structural teaching instead of measuring what he has learnt already.

The procedures seem to be very similar to those of Budoff. Traditional test tasks are used, but each is alternated by a period of teaching. One might say that it is the teachability of the child, rather than his contemporary attainment, that is measured.

THE STUDY OF LEARNING BEHAVIOR

When called into a consultation about a child, the school psychologist requires a means of assessing the child's present functioning in the classroom in order to provide a baseline for the diagnostic/ remedial program. No detailed analysis of cognitive strategies is required. It is not the precise type of thinking, but whether *any* type of thinking occurs that is likely to lead to success in the task and consequent learning. We therefore have to study how the child reacts to the challenge of solving a problem, that is to say, his learning behavior or style of learning.

In his review of the state of thinking about retardation Zigler (1966) prepared the way for this new orientation in assessment. He could not accept the traditional concept of mental deficiency because, as he said, we do not even know what intelligence is. He cites the work of Zeaman and House (1963) and Denny (1964) as demonstrating the crucial importance of attention and motivational variables in learning, as opposed to central deficits of memory or the cognitive structures. In their article on early detection of learning problems, Keogh and Becker (1973) review a further body of work showing that observation of the child's learning behavior by teachers is more accurate in predicting later school achievement than assessments by psychologists or pediatricians using standard tests. They advocate the inclusion of systematic observation of classroom behavior and analysis of children's problem-solving styles as one of the main procedures of assessment.

The importance of studying the child's learning behavior was impressed upon me in the course of my work with slow readers (Stott, 1964). It became quite evident as I got to know these children as individuals that the cause of their reading failure was not mental dullness, but an inability to apply their capabilities to the learning process. Their faulty learning styles either reflected some maladjustment in their general behavior or a specific blockage or inhibition reserved for the learning process itself. The latter were seen to be strategies, albeit unconsciously applied, for the avoidance of a form of activity that had become associated with failure.

The first prerequisite for the success of a remedial program is therefore to identify these inappropriate learning behaviors with a view to correcting them. At the Center for Educational Disabilities at the University of Guelph, systematic observations were carried out on some 250 kindergarten children referred by their teachers as having learning problems. The most obvious types of faulty learning behavior, which reappeared in case after case, were those associated with handicaps of temperament. Among the commonest of these is unforthcomingness, one of the core syndromes of the Bristol Social Adjustment Guides (Stott and Marston, 1970). It is described in the following terms:

> The child fears new tasks or strange situations, and is timid with people while maintaining a need for affection. As a relief from anxiety about school learning the child may accept the role of being 'dull'.

In the manual to the BSAG (Stott, 1974) it is suggested that this temperamental handicap may be a deficiency of effectiveness-motivation. It is seen as a lack of determination to overcome natural apprehensiveness about what is unknown or does not afford certainty of success. Children of this type often use the strategy of giving a tentative half-answer and awaiting the adult's confirmation if correct, or silence if wrong, thus getting the adult to provide the answer for them. Equally common is the temperamental handicap termed "inconsequence" in the BSAG and described as:

> A failure to inhibit first impulses for long enough for their consequences to be foreseen. The child seeks unthinkingly to gain attention, to dominate over his age-peers and to create an impression by showing off. In his school work he is apt to guess rather than take time to work out thoughtful solutions.

The remaining three core syndromes of the BSAG—withdrawal, depression, and hostility—were similarly reflected in characteristic faulty learning styles. Although there is probably always some initial vulnerability of temperament underlying these three forms of maladjustment, to a greater or lesser degree they are brought on by adverse experiences. In the case of hostility, it is probably the result of the child's lack of faith in the continuance of his parents' protection and love. Depression may be the result of lack of sleep, exposure to a highly disorganized home environment, or chronic ill-health.

Whether constitutional within the child or environmentally induced, these general forms of behavior disturbance rank among the originating causes of the learning failure. There are, of course, a host of other originating causes, from physiological damage or maldevelopment of the brain structures to an array of socio-economic/cultural disadvantages in the form of traditional lifestyles that are incompatible with the work-habits demanded in school. A number of other factors external to the child may cause bewilderment and discouragement, notably removal to an unfamiliar human environment, frequent changes of school, and parental anxiety and pressure.

All the above are termed "originating causes," in the sense that they are antecedent to and calculated to produce faulty learning attitudes. If any of them is operating strongly enough to seriously hinder the child's learning, a secondary, reactive type of cause emerges. The experience of failure generates avoidance reactions, which take various forms according to the child's temperament and cultural background. Where the child is apprehensive by nature or his family tradition is one of caution and withdrawal, his defense is likely to be one of playing dull, which is often mistaken for mental slowness. Where the child is by temperament impulsive or an impulsive extraversion is part of his cultural tradition, he is likely to resort to distractibility as a task-evading strategy. Where a child has natural charm, besides suffering some originating handicap or disadvantage, he may turn it to the avoidance of learning situations. A child may resort to sudden wild outbursts as a means of preventing himself from thinking about poignant domestic events, and by antagonizing the bewildered teacher he may start a vicious circle of mutual rejection during which his learning suffers.

Fourteen of these faulty learning styles have been identified and incorporated into the *Guide to the Child's Learning Skills,* which is reproduced as Appendix A to this text. (A fifteenth category, "Doesn't seem aware of what the task calls for," was added to cover those cases in which the child genuinely appeared to the teacher as "just dull." The latter concept is of a state, and not of a style or form of learning behavior.)

It should be emphasized that these fourteen categories are strictly nothing more than descriptions of inappropriate behavioral strategies within the learning situation. Although there is some correspondence with the underlying causes, it is by no means exact. A child's refusal to commit himself to an answer may be a reflection of his constitutional unforthcomingness or may be part of his cultural tradition. His distractibility and disruptiveness may be attributable to a physiologically based hyperactivity and impulsivity, an over-insistent effectiveness-motivation, or a defense against the prospect of failure. As Walker did in exploring the reasons for hyperactivity, we have to look beyond the presenting behavioral symptoms. Where their causes are external to the child, or were once internal but have subsequently ceased to operate, we may expect the inappropriate learning behavior to respond to a conditioning program. Hence the rapidity of the response to remediation acts as a diagnostic pointer, in that it narrows down the possible reasons for the learning failure. The diagram in Figure 1 has been drawn up from this writer's personal experience as an illustration of a composite hypothesis about underlying causes.

Faulty learning behaviors

A B C D E F G H J K L M N O P

Response to reinforcement of good learning behaviors	Rapid	Slow but significant	Poor or none
Hypotheses about origin of low attainment	i. Cultural incompatibility	i. Temperamental handicap	i. Severe temperamental handicap
	ii. Incompatibility of social learning experiences	ii. Neurological dysfunction	ii. Severe neurological dysfunction
	iii. Unfortunate school experiences (changes of school, bad teaching, etc.)	iii. Avoidance due to traumatically painful learning experiences	iii. Chronic ill-health (poisoned tonsils, adenoids, etc.)
		iv. (In older child) Avoidance due to long experience of failure (retreat into incompetence, distractibility, etc.)	iv. Exhaustion, lack of sleep
			v. Hostility (motivation towards disapproval)
			vi. Continued reinforcement of faulty learning style

Figure 1. Behavioral pointers to diagnosis of learning difficulty.

31

TEACHER OBSERVATION OF LEARNING SKILLS

In contrast to the old procedure in which the child is handed over to the psychologist for assessment, under the new orientation the teacher supplies the essential data for the understanding of the immediate causes of the learning failure in the form of observation of the child's learning skills. Needless to say, in making such observations teachers should use systematic methods of reporting, worded in a style that is meaningful to them. Such reports should be of the child's actual behavior and attitudes when faced with learning tasks. The fashionable terminology to which teachers are inclined to resort, such as perceptual problems, hyperactivity, and short attention span, should be discouraged. The psychologist does not require a ready-made diagnosis, but rather a description of how the child copes within a learning situation. The regular procedure, upon a child's being referred, would be for the psychologist to hand the teacher a reporting form, such as the *Guide to the Child's Learning Skills*. The teacher should then be allowed a week or so to re-observe the child's learning behavior with reference to the descriptions given on the Guide. Therapy begins from that point of time. By being induced to study the child's manner of learning—or, more likely, of not learning—the teacher already begins to see what is wrong. By conceiving of the child's difficulties in terms about which something positive might be done, the teacher is no longer driven to frustration and its concomitant avoidance reactions. On the next visit the psychologist should run over the items that have been marked as applying to the child, and he should encourage the teacher to amplify them with further observations that may describe the child more accurately or that may exemplify the faulty learning behavior. At the same time, the psychologist is able to check that the teacher has interpreted the wording of the Guide correctly. The initial working assessment, with regard to the faults in the child's learning attitude that require remediation, is arrived at jointly by the psychologist and the teacher. Subsequently, when it is a question of understanding how these faults have arisen, the psychologist may have to conduct independent investigations and use his own judgement. The psychologist should always refrain from communicating diagnoses, such as "low intelligence" or specific deficits, because they might prompt the teacher to regard the child's failure as inevitable and irremediable.

Diagnosis emerges progressively from working with the child. It is soon seen whether the faulty learning style is just a matter of habit, arising from the manner of the child's upbringing and his cultural tradition, or whether it is part of his temperamental make-up, which may in turn be related to or associated with neurological damage or dysfunction. In the first case, experience shows that the child, however disadvantaged he may be, is able to adapt and extend his behavioral repertoire to new needs, and that he is able to do so with surprising rapidity. Second, the response to remediation may be slow, but it is seldom negligible. The remedial program will reveal what flexibility and adaptability these intrinsically handicapped children may possess. It may be that the neural structures governing the behavioral system are too undeveloped or damaged for us to make any progress with the child towards the adoption of better learning skills, or that, even after he has been trained in such skills, he cannot learn because of some cognitive deficit. However, at least we shall have reached this conclusion after having explored all the remediable alternatives for bringing his potentiality into use.

ADMINISTRATIVE ADVANTAGES

Apart from its logic, such a diagnostic/remedial procedure has administrative advantages. First, productive action can be initiated with relatively little involvement of the psychologist's time. Consequently there is a better chance of reducing, or, ideally, eliminating, the long waiting lists that can make referral a farce. Moreover, as teachers become more used to thinking in terms of poor learning skills, they will be able to handle the behavioral part of the remediation without referral, and call in the psychologist only for the minority of children who do not respond.

The second administrative advantage of the proposed program is that it offers an assessment procedure for special education that relies not on the indirect indications of tests but upon how the child fares in successive treatments, beginning within the regular class. If the curriculum allows members of the class to work in small groups at their own pace, activities appropriate to the level of the slower-learning children can be provided without singling them out with a different program.

THE VICES OF COMPROMISE

Many psychologists will recognize in the concepts and proposals put forward in this book changes that have been taking place for several years. Nevertheless, the adoption of the new approaches has been uneven. Most school psychologists try to achieve a compromise with the traditional psychometric practices. Reasonable as such a compromise may appear, it has resulted in the ineffectiveness that comes from trying to follow two divergent roads at once; the psychologist just does not have the time to carry out formal procedures for testing and also to diagnose and remedy failure in terms of learning skills, not to mention the time needed for the individual casework required by the more serious cases. Moreover, by the continued use of mental tests he is willy-nilly fortifying a conception of mental function that is inimical to a realistic exploration of the causes of learning failure.

I am aware that advocating the complete abandonment of mental measurement may be castigated as an extreme position, but there comes times in the history of civilizations when the complete abandonment of a technology—such as that of bleeding or the practice of witchcraft—is a prerequisite for the adoption of new methods. A further institutional barrier to change is the retention of traditional psychometric techniques in training programs for school psychologists in order to meet the requirements of accreditation, or, in default of such, general expectations about the professional competencies of school psychologists. Consequently, because professionals require a technology, and academics a body of knowledge, to communicate, the new methods must be both elaborated, and seen to be based upon a comprehensive and acceptable theory of learning and learning failure, before the present illogical compromise position can be abandoned.

INCONSISTENT USE OF PSYCHOLOGICAL SERVICES

The diagnostic-remedial procedures described in this book have their justification in the first place in the need to systematize the referral and remediation of children with learning difficulties in order to ensure that none remain in a state of educational neglect. As things are, it is left to the teacher to decide whether or not to report such children to the principal with a view to having him call in the psychologist. If the teacher is inclined to accept the learning

failure of a proportion of the children in his or her class as reflecting an inevitable quota of dullness, natural laziness, or adverse
home influences, about all of which nothing can be done, the
school psychologist and the social worker will be seldom consulted.
Similarly, if the principal has lost faith in the psychological service
or doesn't believe in psychology, few referrals will be made from
that school. In practice it is found that the use of a psychological
service by schools is extremely variable. This is an illogical position:
either the service is not meeting the needs of schools and should be
remodeled, or, if it is effective, every child in every school who
needs it should share its benefits. Although it is hard to generalize
without a survey of the incidence of and reasons for referral, I
suspect that the psychological service is typically called in when a
child shows a combination of learning failure and disturbed behavior that is annoying, baffling, or otherwise upsetting to the
teacher. The attitude of the teacher is that the psychologist will "tell
us what's wrong with him" or, it is hoped, advise the removal of the
child to another educational setting. This attitude makes referral
an avoidance mechanism on the part of the teacher, that is to say,
an escape from a situation that has brought frustration and defeat.

The proposed model for the work of a psychological service
would reverse this state of affairs. Every school would be expected
to use it for the systematic identification of children who are falling
behind their year-group and for the regular review of those earlier
identified. In the great majority of cases referral would not result
in the removal of the child. It is suggested below that the
diagnostic/remedial process should be staged in a way that the most
normal, unobtrusive expedients, involving the minimum segregation of the slower learning child from his peers, would first be tried
(although where the need for it is proved we should not shrink
from segregation). Thus the main responsibility for the remediation would remain with the referring teacher, working in a professional partnership with the psychologist. The latter contributes his
own expertise in the form of specialist knowledge of the cognitive
processes and their motivation, together with the application of this
knowledge in remedial procedures. Therefore, while respecting
the professional experience of the teacher, he acts as consultant
and adviser. The teacher does not give up responsibility for a child
until every possible resource of remediation within the regular
classroom has been exhausted.

CHAPTER SIX

Remediation

The Germans
—and herein they do not stand alone—
possess the gift of rendering the sciences inaccessible.
Men are scared at finding the truth is so simple.
They should bear in mind
that they will be kept quite busy enough
applying it to their practical needs.
J. W. Goethe

The remedial program I am proposing has three objectives. The first is the correction of the child's faulty learning style, the second is intensive tuition in the basic scholastic skills to enable him to catch up with his peers and to resume his place in the regular classroom, and the third encompasses the diagnosis of the reasons for the development of the faulty learning style as well as efforts to eliminate, counteract, or manage them.

CONDITIONING IN LEARNING SKILLS

The correction of the faulty learning behavior is basically one of conditioning. When the child is extremely disturbed and nothing else avails, externally administered rewards, as used in orthodox behavior modification, may be necessary; however, once reinforcements, which form no integral part of the learning process, are discontinued, as they have to be eventually, the motivation to learn may collapse. It is far better that the rewards be inherent in the learning process itself. The child is then able to see the result of his response immediately as it is made. If it is successful, he will be more likely to use the same procedure again. If attending behavior is rewarded by success, and non-attending by failure, the child spontaneously begins to learn the value of attending. In the earliest tasks a mere modicum of attention is required. For example, in the posting of the letter-cards in the Mail Boxes [one of the items of the Flying Start program (Stott, 1971)] the child needs only to match the letter on the card with that on the box, a discrimination task

37

which is within the capacity of young retardates (Clarke and Blake-more, 1961). Once the child has learned the strategy of attending, the complexity of the task can be progressively increased, to the extent that even a very handicapped child may reveal a surprising reserve of concentration. In the Matchers game, one of the later stages of the Flying Start program, the child has to judge by three criteria if he wishes to be certain of making the correct choice. This involves witholding his response to allow time for a sequence of cognitive processes to occur.

With the unforthcoming child, the task at the beginning has to be so obvious and so easy that he can see the solution before he has time to become apprehensive. He then requires a fairly long experience of tasks that are well below his current capacity in order to condition him to an expectation of success. A certainty of success is needed for some types of disadvantaged children, especially those from an ethnic minority, because their culture has trained them to avoid, rather than to tackle, anything that appears difficult.

UTILIZING OUR KNOWLEDGE OF MOTIVATION

Because children who have experienced learning difficulties have often been negatively conditioned, the reconditioning that we plan for them must include learning to enjoy learning. This requirement forces us to draw upon what knowledge we have about the types of activity from which children derive enjoyment in everyday life. In the chapter on motivation I reported an analysis, based on the study of the behavior of my son as a young child, of the features that make for enjoyment in children's play. These provide us with criteria for designing learning materials. The underlying principle of the criteria is that whatever a child does he gains from it some enhancement of his self-image in terms of effectiveness. Each particular achievement can be quite elemental—fitting parts of something together, discriminating between shapes, completing a pattern or an arrangement, matching similar objects, and, as an over-all reinforcement, realizing that he is correct and has succeeded. An important feature of every activity is that, to confer this enhancement, the child should see it as an achievement, that is to say, it should represent an advance upon what he is wont to do. If it is too easy, it will add nothing to his self-image; if he sees it as too difficult, he will shy away from it.

In our remedial treatment we tend to forget that success should be child-perceived rather than teacher-perceived. If a teacher says to a child, "Read this word"—that is, sets him a task in pursuance of his or her teacher-goals—and the child duly reads it, he is unlikely to get any elevation of the spirit. He is not enjoying his success. He is merely meeting the demand that the teacher has made on him. The most he gets is feelings of adequacy and of having got over that hurdle, a relief from tension only until the adult asks the next question. Thus it is not a matter of success irrespective of the task. That chosen by the adult may not be accepted by the child as offering an effectiveness-enhancing prospect. We tend to assume that a child will always make an effort at a solution out of compliance with our wishes. If, as is often the case in a test, the problem is too near the limit of his current capability, he may see in it only the threat of failure, and resort to a well-practiced strategy for opting out. This can be misconstrued as dullness or some mysterious learning disability. Many children retreat into dullness or retardation as a form of avoidance, and naturally enough they get low IQ scores.

The theme of this book is that development of capabilities comes through their use. We cannot command this use. We can command rote learning, or the doing of exercises, or the completing of workbooks, but we cannot command learning as such. We have no alternative but to arrange situations in which learning is likely to occur. This task requires a whole new technology of teaching.

LEARNING GAMES

We are still infected by the traditional dichotomy between work and play. Work could not at the same time be play. Play was the enemy. A child had to be dragged from play to his lessons. The playing child was an idling child, like a machine lying unused. It was overlooked that in their play children work harder, attend more closely, and think more than in a formal lesson. It is this intensity of motivation that our new technology has to learn to evoke.

In their recent book, Bruner and his co-authors (1976) provide us with an insightful analysis of the educative value of play. The first point they make is that it is the actual process of play—the absorption in the activity itself—that is rewarding and enjoyable. They expressed amazement at the time children will spend at their play without any problems of distractibility or short attention span. They noted the freedom from anxiety. As Makins (1976) puts it, "An important thing about play is the way it frees people from tension and alarming consequences." Not winning in one turn just means a postponement of reinforcement until the next (and we know that intermittent reinforcement is more powerful than constant reinforcement). In the course of a game a child can tackle a difficulty in his own time. By a process of what Bruner calls observational learning, he can capitalize upon other children's attempts or explore a problem without committing himself until he feels confident of success. Bruner was struck by the success children achieved in problems that were at first too difficult for them.

In their recent book on hyperactivity, Dorothea and Sheila Ross (1976) recommend small-group games as "providing excellent contexts for attention training as well as for presenting academic and other material." A further advantage of such, they point out, is the amount of repetition that can occur without loss of interest. Even when another child is having his turn a child can rehearse the answers, and so provide himself with a self-learning experience.

In education we have traditionally had a wealth of theoreticians, but few of them were willing to translate their theories into classroom practice. In her review of the above-mentioned book by Bruner and his co-authors, Makins noted that "we have found it remarkably difficult to harness children's play to the business of learning, and those who have succeeded have been less successful in passing on their skills." It is not easy to design learning games, and the attempts of teachers to do so, in the form of simple competitions to proffer the right answers, only have the effect of encouraging the forward and discouraging the slow and the nervous. It was the rash acceptance of an undertaking to teach ten illiterate youths that forced me to resort to games in order to induct them into a first understanding of phonics (they refused point blank to open a book, on the grounds that they were "non-verbal"). The result was a graduated series of group reading games published as the Programmed Reading Kit (Stott, 1962).

In analyzing the reasons for reading failure in the course of remedial work with younger children, it was borne in upon me that, whatever the ultimate causes might be, the link between these reasons and the poor performance was a faulty use of his mental capabilities by the child. Indeed, the only children with whom my colleagues and I failed were those whom we had not been able to persuade to bring their capabilities into play (Stott, 1964). The next step was therefore to identify the most common faulty learning habits and to develop materials specifically designed to correct them. The Flying Start Learning-to-Learn Kits that were the result of this phase of our work consisted of individual and group games that are largely self-correcting.

It was found that the self-correcting feature of the games became a practical necessity if the program was to be used under ordinary classroom conditions. Even in a small remedial or special-education group, children can be at very different stages of attainment and understanding. In these circumstances teacher-centered learning is inefficient, whether the group is taught as a whole or one by one, because in either case each child benefits from the attention of the teacher for only a small fraction of the time. In a regular class of 30 or so, the amount of individual time that can be devoted to each child amounts to only a few minutes per day. If, on the other hand, the teacher can arrange a number of group-learning activities in which each child's response is self-correcting or corrected within the group, every member of the class can be actively learning for the whole time.

This self- and peer-correcting strategy has other advantages. The child does not have to answer to an adult who is "both judge and jury" (Coleman, 1967). Merely being called upon by an adult to give an answer or to solve a problem can produce an inhibition of mental function in anxious children, and in others a defensive avoidance in the form of distractibility or playing dull. Moreover, some children maintain their poor performance in order to command the continued attention of the adult. In an individually solved puzzle or in a game among children, the anxiety is unnecessary and the stalling strategy pointless. Finally, it is inherent in the nature of a game that the players receive immediate knowledge of the outcome of their play, and this is the prime prerequisite for natural learning.

REMEDIATION OF LAGS IN BASIC SKILLS

The second aspect of remediation—that of helping the child to catch up in the basic skills—can only be dealt with by reference to the methods of teaching used. The same conditions for learning apply as were outlined in the learning-to-learn program, namely, an immediate knowledge of outcome, providing for success in terms of the child's own sense of his effectiveness, the maximum possible use of game-like activities, and careful gradation of tasks.

Nevertheless, a knowledge of general learning principles is not enough. When it comes to teaching those children who have failed, it is also a matter of understanding something of the mental processes involved in mastering reading and elementary mathematics. Insufficient attention is given to the teaching of reading in teacher-training programs. Unfortunately, the methods of beginning reading currently most used leave it to the child to organize his own experiences from haphazardly presented material (the excellent verbal short-term memory of most young children can deceive the teacher into believing that genuine reading—in the sense that one group of letters can be distinguished from all other groups of letters—is taking place). The more we leave the structuring of experience to the child, the more we favor those who have the learning skills to carry out such structuring spontaneously. This gives greater advantage to the already advantaged and places more disadvantages in the path of the disadvantaged.

However, it is not just a matter of teaching phonics. The general misunderstanding of the nature of the phonic code has resulted in almost as big mistakes in teaching by phonic methods as were made by attempts to teach reading entirely by sight methods (Stott, 1973a). The most common error is to teach the sounds of the letters in isolation. Away from their word context many of them become mini-syllables that cannot be blended to make words. In so far as a child masters reading through such a presentation of phonics, he has to work out on his own how to encode and decode the true phonemes as they actually occur in words. To achieve this in spite of the presentation of a false code takes up unnecessary time and requires a certain level of learning skill. This misunderstanding of the nature of phonic encoding, and consequent teaching of an artifical code, was one of the reasons why earlier reading specialists insisted that children are not ready to master phonics until they reach a "mental age" of 6–6½ years. It is also the reason for the slow progress in reading of many children at the present time. If the language data are presented in a carefully structured and highly concentrated form, so that it becomes easy for the child to arrive at the letter-sound associations from his own observations, the phonic basis of reading can be systematically taught from the age of five or even earlier.

STAGES OF SPECIAL TREATMENT

It remains to be considered what is the most economical and logical administrative framework for remediation. This is an issue that has been thrown wide open by our querying of the advisability of segregation, and possibly by our going too far in the direction of integration.

It would seem a matter of common sense that the first attempts at remedial treatment should be made within the regular class. Provided the teacher both abandons the objective of trying to keep the whole class advancing through a set syllabus at the same pace and breaks it up, as described in a later chapter, into groups whose size and permanency are determined by the learning needs of each pupil, there is considerable scope for remediation within the regular classroom. This flexibility is enhanced if the curriculum includes self-correcting or peer-correcting activities.

When it becomes apparent that a child requires more intensive help than can be provided in his own classroom, it is obvious that some kind of segregated treatment is indicated. At first the segregation should only be partial, consisting in withdrawal for small-group remedial help for two or three sessions weekly. The lack of specialist resource teachers has struck me as one of the more important gaps in the present Toronto system. The only one I observed showed an extremely uneconomical use of teacher power, namely a one-to-one student/teacher session. Using a game approach and self-correcting learning activities makes possible a ratio of one teacher to six students per session. If the activities promote self-learning this ratio enables the resource teacher to spend time with each group or individual student as necessary. In my early experimental work on withdrawal programs for remedial reading (Stott, 1964) the teachers were able to cope with twelve students at a time, with good results, but this was admittedly hard going. To alleviate the strain, volunteers could well be used as teaching assistants.

Withdrawal for part of the week has been criticized as marking out children as different from their peers. My experience, however, has been that among 8-year-old backward readers there is keen competition to get into such a remedial group. In the above-mentioned experimental work we were often pressured by a principal to make up the group in his school to twelve if any of the original group had a prolonged absence; when the latter returned, the temporary fill-ins refused to be excluded.

There will be a few children within the withdrawal group who fail to respond. These are likely to be those who have such severe handicaps of temperament that they cannot adapt even to small-group learning under specialist supervision, are subject to emotional stresses arising from family problems, are depressed by chronic ill-health or malnutrition, or suffer from a cognitive maldevelopment or damage. Such failure would be an indication for the second stage, i.e., full-time special education and perhaps social-work counseling of the family. It is seen that this empirical manner of selection for special education makes a program of assessement by standard tests redundant. Such a selection method renders special education more effective by progressively identifying those children who show that they really need a sheltered, segregated setting.

ASSISTANCE TO THE TEACHER

Primary school teachers are at a disadvantage in the help they can give to the slower learners in two respects. The first is that their training for the most part has not included the special skills required. A channel must be provided for communicating to them the most effective and up-to-date methods. This can be done by the establishment of local teachers' resource centers, in which instructional materials can be examined and explained, and by a service of specialist advisers visiting the classrooms.

The second difficulty faced by primary teachers is that they have to deal with a bewilderingly wide range of aptitudes, learning skills, and social adjustment, which get progressively ironed out, or sorted out, as the children move up the school. Provided there is not too great a concentration of problems, the exceptional primary teacher can do justice to the needs of the slower learners by careful organization and hard work, of which there were some notable examples in the project. In general, however, one has to say that teachers need assistance at this stage of education if our objective of effective remediation for every child is to be met. This is even more true if the class contains many recent immigrants and other disadvantaged children. It becomes increasingly difficult for the child who has failed to master the basics at the primary stage to catch up in the later stages, and efforts to help him are hindered by his discouragement and his avoidance of the area of failure. A preventive program at the primary stage is therefore the most economical and human way of tackling learning difficulties.

Community volunteers are one such resource of assistance, but skill is required in using this resource. Generally, the mobilization of a few mothers, as was done by one of the teachers in the project, makes an auspicious beginning, but such volunteers tend to be irregular and to fall away in the course of the year. The successful volunteer programs I have known have been energetically organized by the principal as a community project involving a fairly large number of adults. The principals in question have emphasized to me the danger of issuing public calls for volunteers; they should be handpicked from the community by the teaching staff. Mr. Dan Rainey of the Pinecrest Memorial School in Prince Edward County, Ontario, has evolved a model community-volunteer program, the features of which bear propagation. Its organizer is a retired teacher who is paid on a part-time basis by the School Board (cost $2,000 per school per year). The parent and other volunteers are recruited for a 12-week program of two 45-minute sessions per week. This limited commitment enables the volunteers to discontinue at the end of the period without letting the teacher down, and can be a tactful way of not re-inviting a volunteer who proves unsuitable. A further prerequisite is a meticulously structured program of teaching activities and a means by which the regular teacher can check the children's progress session by session. In order to avoid the pressures of straight one-to-one teaching, the use of game techniques is also advisable. A well-planned learning game prescribes a teaching procedure that is independent of the volunteer.

Another source of assistance used at the Pinecrest School, and also in two schools within the project, was that of older students from the same school to help in the primary class. One of the psychologists involved in the Toronto project also trained a group of six from the special-education class in the use of the learning games, and they operated successfully throughout its course. In another school, three bright sixth grade students were recruited from a special individualized curriculum for 30-minute sessions every other day. Each of them was able to cope with five Grade One children. To those who question the withdrawal of older children from their lessons to act as teaching assistants may be quoted the old adage that the best way to learn is to teach. It has also been observed, especially with older boys who are drifting without a sense of purpose, that being given the responsibility of helping to teach younger children has a salutary effect on their self-image and social attitudes.

DEALING WITH ULTIMATE CAUSES

The third aspect of remediation consists in removing, so far as may be, the original causes of the learning failure. The observation of a faulty learning style is of value not only in providing a baseline for a corrective program, but also, as indicated above, in affording pointers to underlying causes. Any initial diagnosis, by observation or by test, can only be tentative, in that it provides us with only one or more hypotheses. At the risk of being repetitious it must be emphasized that similar symptoms presented in the form of inappropriate learning behaviors may arise from very different causes. Understanding of these symptoms develops in the course of work with the child on a program designed to remedy the faulty approach to learning. When a child does not respond to the conditioning process, a great deal of clinical time may have to be spent in interviews with parents, visits to the home, obtaining medical reports, and so on. This type of intervention becomes an important part of the work of the school psychological, psychiatric, and social-work services. Although these professional skills are outside the scope of this text, I have not been able to refrain from offering some counsel (Chapter Ten) about the kinds of family situations that tend to generate hostile attitudes.

CHAPTER SEVEN

Review
of
The Children
Referred in
The
Toronto Project

*A happy child
will always learn
and hear.*
Geoffrey Chaucer

After having established the fact of learning failure, the first diagnostic step is to ascertain the child's style of learning, or more accurately, of non-learning. This shows us why the necessary mentation is not occurring, that is to say, in what way the cognitive system is in a state of dysfunction. Until we can get the system functioning by a program designed to correct the faulty learning behavior, we are not justified in diagnosing any structural deficit. A typology of learning style therefore affords us not only a convenient form of initial classification but also an indication of the remediation needed for each child. Consequently, in reviewing the cases dealt with in the Toronto project, I shall group them in the first place by learning style.

The first group, of 13 children, could have been given the all-too-fashionable label "hyperactive." On the *Guide to the Child's Learning Skills,* they received marks for "Acts without taking time to look or work things out," "Easily distracted," "Looks for ways of evading learning tasks," etc. They would have been likely candidates for drug treatment. If this had happened, they would never have learned to control their impulsivity by natural means. In fact, five of them responded so well to the Flying Start Learning-to-Learn and basic skills programs that they were cured of their faulty learning habits and could take their place in the regular work of the class. Typical teachers' remarks were: "Took time to deliberate and made good choices," "Progressed marvellously," "No longer a problem," "Acquired good work habits, 100 per cent improved." The impulsivity of four was only partly overcome. One of these "succeeded as long as he made sure," but did very well with the early phonics materials (Things Alive). Another reached a typical halfway-point: he was able to concentrate while in a small group with the teacher but not while working alone. For this boy, continuance for a time in a special program is indicated. The two others made good progress, but one entered the program only in January (halfway through its course), and the other had only a small exposure to the materials, besides entering a month late. The last two, together with the first five, showed such rapid change for the better in their learning style as to suggest that their initial poor learning skills were a culturally transmitted lifestyle, or the result of their never having been in a situation where reflectivity offered advantages. Four of them—one of whom was described as a "proper little hellion"—had had little or no previous experience of school. The whole of the credit for their improvement cannot therefore be given to the project, because they would no doubt have settled down sooner or later in any case. Nevertheless, there are obvious advantages in this happening sooner and as the result of a planned program of remediation aimed at the source of the learning difficulty.

The program revealed that the remaining four hyperactive children had an intrinsic temperamental problem with concentration and impulsivity. They seemed to answer to the classic pattern of hyperactivity of neurological origin. Two had a slight speech defect and another was motor-impaired. Nevertheless, three of them learned to concentrate in the Flying Start activities, although this did not carry over to their general learning. The indication for all four was a period of special education.

Four other children could have been categorized as hyperactive, but their handicap of temperament—if it can be so called—was a high effectiveness-motivation that clashed with the classroom routine. The first, a Black boy, was creative in his artwork and showed powers of leadership. In learning situations "he had to be totally right." In particular, he could not tolerate the unstructured sentence method of teaching beginning reading, and became increasingly antagonistic to this and to the teacher. When given the phonic clues in the project games, he did exceedingly well. A high-effectiveness Italian girl was described by her teacher as "a strong, independent personality." She was so contrasuggestive that she took a pride in getting things wrong. She would not accept any activity she did not choose herself, but she could organize a group well and liked to be in charge. She was usually the one who acted as teacher in the Things Alive phonics game, and the one who checked on the Number Wheels (for a systematic description of the remedial materials, see Appendix B). These opportunities to take the leader role meant that she did well in the project activities. An Italian boy expressed his need for effectiveness by bullying other children, or by playing the clown and making them laugh. By the end of the project, however, the teacher was able to report, "He has become keen on his work. He attacks a problem correctly the first time; previously, he guessed." And "he has become a lot more tame in relations with other children. He is not a real behavior problem now. He can stick at a task for half an hour even if it's boring." The fourth was described by his teacher as "hyperactive, impetuous and very talkative." He had little concentration because he always had something important to say. With his active mind, and being the son of professional parents, he had a vocabulary and style of speaking much above his years. At first he was unable to restrain his eagerness in the project games, but later he learned to work in a disciplined way. It became evident that none of these four children needed anything more than a program that satisfied their high effectiveness-needs while letting them see that they could do this best by learning to control their behavior.

The next group to be considered were nine unforthcoming children. The description typically given of them was, "You have to coax every answer out of him; afraid to say the answer." When pressed, the children might make a slow, hesitant guess, or wait for a cue from the teacher. They gave the appearance of being duller than they really were, and at least one of this group showed by the intelligent and creative way in which he handled the play activities that he was reserving his dullness for formal learning situations. If the work was new or appeared too lengthy, he would just give up. He did very well at the Flying Start and beginning phonics activities. Another child had a WISC performance score of 72, but his teacher said: "I wouldn't go along much with the low IQ, I wouldn't agree with it. He is super-shy. He has to be sure he's right."

In all these nine cases the unforthcomingness seemed to be primarily a matter of temperament. How severe a handicap it may be can be ascertained only by a program attuned to their lack of confidence, that is to say, providing a carefully planned progression of activities advancing by very easy stages. Once such a child has become conditioned to an expectancy of success his very caution induces him to attend carefully and reflect, so that he develops a good style of learning. This happened with five of the nine unforthcoming children to the extent that they might be expected to follow a regular second grade curriculum. The other four all made some progress with the Flying Start, but the indications were that they would require ongoing special treatment.

There was a further group of eight children showing a mild unforthcomingness, but as part of a characteristic syndrome of other poor learning styles. Their symptoms were: playing dull, slow hesitant guessing on meeting a difficulty, distractibility, looking for ways of evading tasks, and lack of interest or energy. The total picture added up to an avoidance of the challenges of learning. Four of these children had evidently been reduced to this state by parental pressures. They progressed well, one of them resuming work with the regular class as early as January.

Another child had been exposed to extreme parental overprotection. By the end of the project his teacher was able to report a general improvement in his work habits, notably that "He stays with something until he gets it right." The other three children who originally showed this general avoidance syndrome also made good progress both in attainment and in work habits. One was described at the end of the project as still a slow learner, but he was in a class in which the project was started late because of lack of assistance for the teacher. The reasons for their fears and bewilderment seemed to be mainly cultural, with the addition in one case of lack of previous schooling. In sum, none of this group evidenced a need for continued special education, except possibly the last-mentioned.

A group of three children showed avoidance symptoms in the form of lack of concentration, day-dreaming, and passivity. All had been subject to neglect, social stress, or insensitive treatment in their homes. The first of these did well on the Flying Start, but we were unable to observe his further progress because in January he returned to his previous school. The second was in one of the classes where the project could not be put into effect regularly because of lack of assistance for the teacher, but the latter said of him, "Academically he has surprised me. He is slow but he learns what he's supposed to learn." One had developed the most severe avoidance strategies. His dullness and lethargy were so extreme that the teacher could get a mere one-word answer out of him only by repeated prodding. When he was asked a question his eyes would turn away in a far-off look. On the Mail Boxes of the Flying Start he started by posting in a "don't care" manner, but he quickly became competitive and succeeded well. Nevertheless, he maintained his lethargic, don't-care stance, and we began to suspect a health problem. In an interview, his mother described symptoms that suggested that he had had chronic middle-ear infections for many years, but his family doctor examined him and found nothing wrong. An older brother said that at home his mother threatened to set the police on him if he didn't learn at school. Our tentative diagnosis was that his lethargy and avoidance were attributable to a combination of poor health and anxieties produced by insensitive attitudes at home. In the course of the project he reached a stage where he would participate willingly, but he slumped into his lethargic state as soon as no demands were made on him. However, I was able to observe him, towards the end of the project, playing with the Things Alive Cards in a group of children under the leadership of an older special-education student. He was attending well, and when his turn came he was able to pick the *d* for *dog* correctly from among nine cards which included *b*, *d*, and *q*. It was clear that in these three cases the need was as much for social-work help in the home as for special education.

Cognate with the above extreme withdrawal strategies was the elective mutism of one girl. By visiting her home and by progressively extending the range of people with whom she would talk, the psychologist was successful in getting her to speak normally in school. There were no doubt good reasons discoverable within her family life for her deciding not to speak, but it was outside the scope of the project to investigate them.

Two boys expressed their family problems in school by hostility. The parents of both urgently required social-work counseling or some similar service provided by the school; however, the boys left the school during the project. There is no doubt that the frequent changes of school suffered by children from unstable families are a major contributing factor in both emotional and attainment deficits.

Three children exhibited Pattern L of the Guide—exploiting charm or a handicap to avoid learning. A Japanese girl with a vision and speech problem fastened on counting as her favorite disability; however, she could do additions when using the Addition Mail Boxes and the Clothes Pegs, although she treated the former as a joke at first. The teacher complained that her peculiarity was that she had to start right at the beginning again each year, which suggested the strategy of using a learning problem as a means of getting attention. Two West Indian girls were adept at relying on their charm to get help, although in their chosen activities they were competent enough. One of them left at Christmas, but by March the other could write stories with the use of a picture dictionary, while still using her helplessness ploy in mathematics. This charm-plus-stupidity strategy would be reinforced if the child were placed in a low-achieving special group. It should be sufficient for the psychologist to recognize it and to make sure that it is not reinforced by being taken at its face value. The best antidote is to involve the child in games that contain peer-correcting components. Children who use the playing-stupid attitude with adults are seldom willing to appear helpless before their peers, nor can they trade on their charm.

Three children answered to the don't-care attitude of Pattern J, but for different reasons. One, a boy from the West Indies, approached the teacher with an expectation of race prejudice and could talk intelligently on the subject. Like the Black boy mentioned above, he had an intense dislike of sight-reading methods, but he did well with a phonic approach. The two others combined a lack of interest in achievement with aggressiveness towards other children. They both did well in the project, and one learned to respond to the discipline of the class, for which the teacher rather than the project must be given credit.

There were three children much handicapped by ill-health and absences. One had the apprehensive, avoiding, guessing, playing-dull syndrome referred to above, but after treatment of her ear in the hospital she became, in the teacher's words, "a brand new child." She did extremely well on the Flying Start and was taken out of the project because she needed no further remedial help.

One last boy, a Canadian Indian, approached every task with the caution characteristic of his culture, but unfortunately the tasks he was set (sight-memory of words) did not provide him with the certainties he required. He insisted on repeatedly coming to the teacher for confirmation, which in the circumstances was a sensible thing to do. He did well on the Flying Start and the Number materials. His was a teaching, rather than a learning, problem.

In assessing the results of the project it should be borne in mind that at the outset neither the teachers nor the psychologists involved in the project were familiar with the remedial materials, and I had to demonstrate these progressively throughout the seven months of its operation (interrupted by the Christmas period). In some classes the remedial program took a long time getting started because the teachers felt that they could not manage without assistance. Consequently, the results of the project in terms of the children's progress could not be taken as a measure of the potential efficacy of the remedial methods used. In effect, of the 50 children picked out by their teachers as educationally high-risk and who had some degree of exposure to the project, 26, as indicated by the teachers' final reports during the March of 1976, had learned to settle down well to their work and were no longer a subject of concern. They were able to keep up with the regular work of the class and no difficulty was anticipated for them in the next grade. Eight children had made progress despite only partial exposure to the project or having entered it late, having left the school in the middle of the year, or having been in one of the classes where it did not become fully operative. Eight others responded well as regards their learning skills considering their handicaps, but they would evidently need special help, either in the regular class or in a remedial group, the following year. A further eight revealed more serious handicaps: they all made some progress but would need intensive special education for the next year or two at least. The effect of the project was to identify them as children with severe learning problems by a method of assessment—exploring their contemporary capabilities and needs in a learning situation—which, it is claimed, must be more accurate and realistic than assessment by tests. At the same time the project served to identify at least half the group, and, if they had spent more time in it, probably another 16%, as children whose learning difficulties were due to environmental disadvantages, not to handicaps. The gratifying aspect of the remediation of the basically normal group was the speed with which they responded to the conditioning in learning how to learn. As reported in Chapter Eleven, Dr. Marie O'Neill (1975) made a similar observation from her experiment in using the Flying Start with junior and senior kindergarten children in Toronto schools.

CHAPTER EIGHT

Assessing The Learning Environment

*It's hard to be modest
when you've got the right biases.*
D. O. Hebb

HOW PERMANENT WILL BE THE GAINS OF INTERVENTION?

The haunting concern of those who engage in remedial teaching is what progress the child will make after his return to the regular class. We cannot brush aside the research results showing that the progress in reading made during remediation tends to fade after the child's return to the regular curriculum (Collins, 1961, and others summarized in Silberberg and Silberberg, 1969). This is not evidence against the value or indeed the necessity of remedial programs in general. Most such programs last too short a time; in the writer's experience many children who have fallen seriously behind or have failed to make a start in reading require help in a small withdrawal group for up to a year. Moreover, we have to be assured that the remedial methods used lead to the mastery of basic concepts that represent permanent gains. It is understandable that remediation consisting of the sight-learning of words will show immediate gains on a word-recognition test but be quickly forgotten for lack of the basic phonic concepts. The remediation may also fail to correct the operational disability of the poor reader, namely his faulty learning skills. The gains may have been made in a one-to-one tuition, which gives no practice in the skills of attending and persevering in a regular class.

THE WRONG LEARNING ENVIRONMENT?

Probably the most general reason for the apparent failure of remediation is that, after making good progress in a remedial group or early-intervention program, the child is exposed to a curriculum that is ill-suited to his needs. He is then all too likely to suffer a slump in confidence and motivation, and revert to one of the self-defeating strategies for avoiding unrewarding learning situations (examples are listed in the *Guide to the Child's Learning Skills* in Appendix A). We have to admit that, as things are, it is a matter of luck whether or not such a child enjoys continuing good conditions for learning. The kind of teaching a child gets is, by common consent, left to the individual teacher. If the teacher, either from intuition or as a result of the requisite training and guidance, provides the right environment for learning, so much the better. However, in teacher training and in our adviser services it would be hard to find clearly formulated guidelines about what constitutes good conditions for learning.

Perhaps the biggest advance in education waiting to be made over the coming generation is the definition of these good conditions for classroom learning and the building upon them of an explicit body of professional practice that can form a major part of teacher training. In short, we have to decide what makes effective teaching.

ATTEMPTS TO COMPARE TEACHING STYLES

It would be premature to attempt at this stage to make formal experimental comparisons between one style of teaching and another. Enormous, and for practical purposes insuperable, methodological difficulties arise when we try to compare the behavior and performance of teachers in across-group experiments (Bannatyne, 1975; Blackman, 1972). One of the biggest problems is ensuring that each group of teachers is adhering to an explicitly defined method, so that we can be sure exactly what we are comparing. Because of neglect of this precaution, the recent research of Bennett (1976) in Britain was virtually meaningless: within the styles of teaching compared, an inconsistent hotchpotch of methods was used. To embark upon the testing of alternative methods before they have been properly worked out and refined in classroom situations is to stand science on its head. All scientific knowledge starts by observing what happens.

> Experimentation is generally the *last* step in the acquisition of knowledge rather than the first. Much theorizing and naturalistic observing

has to be done before worthwhile experiments are possible. The experimenter is the last member of the relay team (Maslow, 1955).

Maslow's counsel was ignored by a generation of educational experimentalists who vied with each other to be more scientific than the scientists. After a spate of results, practically every one of which was contradicted by another, we have arrived back at the point where disciplined and systematic observation is beginning to be accorded its due place.

In the study of the conditions needed for good learning this means a methodology of formative evaluation—observing what works and what doesn't work, and modifying the method progressively until its faults are eliminated. This need not be a subjective or haphazard process. With suitable training, observers should be able to record reliably whether or not learning of the right sort is taking place, as evidenced by the students' absorption in the learning task and the quality of learning achieved.

FORMULATING THE CHARACTERISTICS
OF A GOOD LEARNING ENVIRONMENT

Perhaps the best exercise in formulating a good learning environment is to attempt to draw up what might be called a "Conditions of Learning Assessment Scale," based upon the tapping of teacher experience and what we can glean from studies and theories of learning. The rationale for such an activity is provided by Gagné (1965):

> Learning is not simply an event that happens naturally; it is also an event that happens under certain observable conditions. Furthermore, these conditions can be altered and controlled; and this leads to the possibility of examining the occurrence of learning by means of the methods of science.

I am going to imagine, therefore, that I am in charge of a group of teachers who are in their initial training or are attending a refresher course, and ask myself what criteria they might use for judging whether the classroom environment they observe or create favors good learning. Obviously the emphasis would change somewhat according to the age and capabilities of the students. The criteria would therefore have to be applied with flexibility. Moreover, it would be rash for a single individual to be dogmatic about them, considering the small amount of experience he can have had, compared with that of a host of other teachers. It is as a *starting point* for thinking and observation, therefore, that I suggest the following criteria:

1. Is the process of learning absorbing, rewarding, and enjoyable to the students?

An important point made by Bruner and his co-authors (Sylva, Bruner, and Genova, 1976) in their recent collection of writings on play is that to the child it is the actual process that is rewarding. For this reason even very young children show the most extraordinary absorption and perseverance in their play. We would thus want to observe how many students during a sampled period of time are obviously absorbed in a learning activity with an unforced perseverance and concentration.

I would not award positive absorption marks for situations in which a class of children are apparently listening to or watching a teacher. Children can become adept at sitting still and assuming the expression of attending while their minds are elsewhere, or at attending only to the gestures and vocalizing of the teacher without attempting to follow the explanation. Moreover, explanation to a whole class is usually a waste of time, because the mental activity of working over and testing logically the exposition stage by stage demands an unusually high level both of motivation and of cognitive skill on the part of the explainee. Naturally the efficacy of exposition depends upon the age of the students and their ability to test each point the teacher makes against their own concepts and experience. In general, such an ability is found only in highly selected, academically oriented, older students, and probably even only a minority of college students possess it.

2. Does the student get to know the result of his effort soon enough to look back and note what he did that caused it to be correct or incorrect?

We may call this a criterion of natural learning, because many things are learned in everyday life by noting what works and what doesn't work. We take whatever action seems best to us at the time to achieve a desired solution, and, if our existing understanding of the problem is incomplete, we may have to make a guess at the most promising alternative. If we know whether or not we have chosen correctly while we can still remember what we did, a condition for learning is fulfilled. Let us suppose, for example, a student answers some pages of questions in a workbook, hands them in, and has them returned corrected only the next day, or possibly even later. He will be unlikely to remember the processes by which he worked out the answers. Unless he is motivated much above the average he will not go over all his mistakes to try to reconstruct where he went wrong. This is not to say that workbooks should be banished, but they do lend themselves to mechanical "busywork" activities that are a parody of learning.

3. Is the intended new learning firmly based on previously acquired capabilities?

It is not enough that the whole learning syllabus be logically structured, although this is obviously a prerequisite. The question is rather whether or not the student has integrated the concepts of the earlier stage into his thinking so well that he can use them easily and fluently in the solution of problems at the higher stage. Concepts only become effective tools of thought by being used to get answers. It is at this stage that vagueness, misinterpretation, invalid generalization, incomplete discrimination and the like are revealed and rectified. Concepts are forged on the anvil of use.

How, it may be asked, does the observer who is assessing the quality of a learning environment know if this condition is being fulfilled? Obviously it is of no use to question the student, because he may not know himself whether he has mastered a concept or not. The key to the answer is that thinking is a very rapid process. If a response is based on concepts that have become tools of thought, it will be made rapidly and with certainty. A child who is just beginning to read and who has achieved the concepts of the phoneme/grapheme associations (concepts because they are generalizations from a number of near-similar events) will be able to read unfamiliar syllables without hesitation or the necessity of sounding out, and once the syllables have become conceptualized he will be able to read unfamiliar words (provided they are not too irregular) apparently at sight.

It should be emphasized that the touchstone for this criterion is not whether the student can state the rule, but whether he can operate it. People can, and normally do, integrate concepts into their thinking without being aware of doing so. We use the grammatical rules of our native language, according to the accepted usage of our social group, without recognizing them consciously as rules of grammar. As any perceptive teacher of languages knows, the verbal knowledge of grammatical rules is no guarantee of their correct application. Similarly, an ability to repeat multiplication tables does not confer an understanding of when to multiply or when to divide. A correct programming in arithmetic would arrange for the students to make calculations involving multiplying, and, by discovering what a laborious job it is to count up afresh each time or to keep on adding the same number to the total, to realize that it makes sense to learn the multiplication facts, which then become concepts that have emerged in the course of an activity because they are useful. The student has a capability that he thoroughly understands because he developed it himself. In short, capabilities should be assessed by the ability to use them, as proof of understanding, rather than by the ability to repeat general statements.

4.   Is each student in the group genuinely working at his own level and pace?

However finely classes are streamed, or a class is grouped, by their supposed ability, differences of pace soon emerge. A student who develops motivation, perhaps because he likes the teacher or gets a sudden grasp of the subject, forges ahead rapidly, and, conversely, if he loses his motivation he falls behind. Hence an attempt to keep a class or a group advancing at the same rate through a set syllabus is an inefficient teaching strategy because it provides a poor learning environment for the majority of the class. The effects of their bewilderment and discouragement on the slower learners hardly need to be mentioned, and the effects of boredom, for example, on the rapid learners, especially those who are creative and self-directed, is to turn them off what the school has to offer.

Nevertheless, we have to face the very real fears of teachers both about how to cope with the student who is getting too far ahead, and how to give personal attention to the slower students without neglecting the main body of the class. The type of classroom organization that might meet our criterion and allay these anxieties is a fluid group structure in which groups are formed for specific learning activities or projects. In general the members of any group would be fairly equal with regard to the stage they had reached in the basic skills, but often a more advanced student could be attached temporarily to a slower group as a "teacher." For many activities a group could consist of students of very mixed capabilities, each performing a function at his own level.

5. Does the method of teaching encourage the students to learn by their own mental activity?

Learning is something that the individual has to do for himself. It consists of a series of internal processes: receiving information through the senses, reviewing it mentally in order to decide what may be worth remembering, and then storing it away with similar observations or with whatever was observed to have some sort of association with it. In this way a structure of knowledge arises. The individual in whose brain such events occur acquires a sort of working model of part of the external world, which, by some kind of coding system analogous to, but more complicated than, a computer program, can be made to produce answers in terms of time and space, color, tone, knowledge of human nature, etc. He is then in a position to accept further observations and to fit them into the model. If he succeeds in doing this, we say that he understands something. Only to a very limited extent can items of information be left lying around without being incorporated in a structure; even if they are never completely erased they cannot be retrieved, because the process of remembering would seem to consist in making contact with structures.

The importance of this for the teacher is that information cannot just be shovelled into the learner's brain. As Vygotsky (1962) says, "The direct teaching of concepts is impossible and fruitless." At this point, however, we have to be careful not to jump to the conclusion that the student has to be left to discover every connection himself without help from the teacher. Unfortunately, discovery methods have been made the excuse for just leaving children to make their own sense of a so-called rich learning environment, and this has been confused with a progressive philosophy of education. Left to themselves, many children will be content not to advance to a more efficient coding of information. How many, for instance, would spontaneously make the generalization that 2 and 2 make 4, and then program themselves with the addition facts, let alone the multiplication facts? Even children with active minds who structure their own observations run a risk of doing so incorrectly because they do not have access to a wide enough range of experience or because they have not acquired the supporting concepts that enable them to arrive at a true understanding. When I told my young son that it was of no use to keep the hot tap running because the water was cold, he explained to me that if you put your finger under the running tap it would make the water come hot.

A completely wrong idea can act as a block to further learning because it is of no use for arriving at answers, and the child gets confused and discouraged. If a child thinks counting is just a matter of saying numbers, he cannot understand that the order of the numbers is important and he may change them around just to provide a little variety. Moreover, a child cannot explain that he has a wrong conception, and it may remain unsuspected and undiagnosed for a long time.

In sum, even though we accept the principle that learning can only take place by the learner's own mental activity, the teacher has to facilitate the process and monitor the developing concepts so that they represent true replicas of the outside world. The data of experience have to be presented to the student in a highly selective way that enables him to "put two and two together" correctly. The discovery of the concept has to be guided, perhaps by directing attention to certain essential regularities, by suggesting hypotheses to be tried, and so on (see Gagné, 1965, pp. 268–270)—so long as the student, after taking the hints and following the clues, gets the satisfaction of grasping the idea by coming to it himself. It has to be admitted that to arrange learning situations that meet this criterion calls for a well-developed educational technology. We have to get used to the fact that, as Gagné says, teaching is a very intricate and demanding activity. If we are going to support the intuitive skills of the teacher with an explicit know-how based on learning principles, a great deal of attention will need to be devoted to the design of learning units, and we shall require a profession of teacher-advisers who are trained to act as consultants in their proper use.

6.   Are there opportunities for students to interact socially during the learning process and to learn from each other?

In traditional communities nearly all learning is a social process. The young learn from their elders and each other, first by observation and imitation in games, and eventually by being allowed to take part in the activity. The sociability of a group is in itself a great reinforcer. A face-to-face group meets our instinctive needs as a social species, as is witnessed by the length of time people will remain together at a card game, over social drinking, or even just hanging about in groups. A group imposes a natural discipline on its members. The youngster who behaves irresponsibly in the "crowd" of a class to which he feels no allegiance recognizes, or is made to recognize, that membership in a small group requires him to play his expected part and to put his best foot forward. Group-learning activities also have advantages in overcoming faulty learning habits that are discussed in the next chapter.

The assessor of the learning environment would note first of all how the seating is arranged in the classroom. Is it in neat rows only suitable for attending to the teacher and for individual work? Social psychologists know that the way people are grouped in a given space has a large influence on the way they interact with each other. Formal rows of desks all facing in one direction predetermine lines of interaction between each individual student and the teacher. This sets a pattern for a method of teaching that consists of teacher talking and students listening, or of students all working individually. It virtually precludes the more natural forms of learning that occur within peer groups.

We have to be alert to the danger that the present fashion for individualized learning does not result in the "solitary confinement" of the student by a machine or programmed text. Such social isolation is calculated to have long-term stress effects similar to those of regular work in a windowless room, which induces a kind of deprivation syndrome of which the victim is aware of only as a dislike of the work setting.

It must nevertheless be emphazed that it is not a matter of *either* social *or* individual learning activity. Individual study is often necessary as a contribution to a group project or learning program. The roles within the group are necessarily individual roles. Moreover, a student may often develop an individual interest or just prefer to work alone. He may have the sort of independent temperament that does not need a social stimulus or even resents interference with his self-directed learning interests. Many artistic and other creative individuals are like that. There is room for them in a class working in small groups; they simply form, for their chosen activity, a group of one.

7. Is sufficient time allowed for newly won knowledge to sink in?

It has been shown experimentally that learning needs time to sink in. Events that are considered important are turned over in the mind until they establish firm associations and can be linked to some existing structure of knowledge. After one has had a narrow squeak, say from a skid by driving too fast on a slippery road, the memory returns time and again with an accompanying shudder at the thought of what might have happened. Or, after having said or done something unkind one may experience feelings of remorse, which is a way of learning not to do the same thing again. These are mechanisms of internal conditioning, a recapitulation of the event that causes a single episode to be repeated mentally a number of times. It is obviously a much more economical and efficient way of learning than conditioning by repetition of the actual happening, perhaps up to 30 times, such as Pavlov found to be necessary in teaching animals to connect two events, although it is now recognized that animals also can learn from single episodes, presumably by the same kind of mental recapitulation that humans use.

The important thing is that this mulling-over needs time. If the process is thrown into confusion by presentation of further material of a similar kind (retroactive inhibition) the learning of the original material cannot be completed. Retroactive inhibition is only one way of interfering with the completion of learning. Any necessity to give attention to a fresh topic immediately after a learning experience will interfere with its completion. Especially in the latter stages of schooling, students tend to be rushed from one lesson to another in a way that must prevent the learning that has occurred in the earlier lessons from sinking in. When, in the early stages of my professional career, I was interviewed for the headship of a secondary school, I put forward this idea and suggested that between each lesson students should be allowed a ten-minute quiet do-as-you-please time. The appointing body evidently thought this was too radical an idea, because I was not offered the job. It is not necessarily the best way of ensuring a sinking-in interval, but some such is necessary for effective permanent learning. It is probably rather artificial to try to program learning-consolidation intervals, but when the teaching involves a great deal of formal exposition they must surely be helpful. It should be added that an interval of boisterous physical activity could well have the same interfering effect as any other period of intense concentration.

In a learning game this problem doesn't arise. The significant learning events tend to be spaced out sufficiently for each to be incorporated into the permanent register of stored knowledge. If the student is gathering information by himself from reading, discussion, or observation, he will likewise have time for mulling over. The real danger of the erasure of learning occurs in a multi-stage explanation, or working through stage after stage of a programmed text. On the other hand, exercises directly related to some new learning experience, even of a mechanical character, may be a good way of consolidating the knowledge, provided they don't offend against the next criterion, which is the avoidance of monotony.

8. Are the learning situations sufficiently varied?

This criterion has two aspects. The first derives from the reason why we like variety in anything. It stems from the universal need for some degree of effectiveness in dealing with our environment. We are reinforced, and get feelings of self-enhancement, if we find that we can do something we couldn't do before, or understand something that was previously baffling. Leading thinkers are now suggesting that the basic urge to learn and understand is an aspect of effectiveness-motivation (Bruner, 1966, pp. 114–119; Zigler, 1970, p. 104). A central feature of this source of motivation is that after a while the child exhausts the possibilities for effectiveness that any one activity can offer. Once he can do something easily he gets no further feelings of increased competence by continuing to do it. A novel play activity will be approached with caution, then—with the flush of first mastery—it is intensively exploited, until quite suddenly it is abandoned. The child may come back to it momentarily after a little while, but he quickly realizes that it is "old hat" and drops it after a brief retrial (Stott, 1961). Wilenski (1927), the well-known art theoretician of the previous generation, pointed out that one gets tired of even the best pictures with long enough exposure to them because the possibilities of discovery that they can offer are limited. With repeated playing, a piece of music can become not only boring but maddening.

Consequently we have to ask to what extent the sameness of the learning materials used in schools can become boring and—to those with a high effectiveness-motivation—maddening (see the section on the creative child in Chapter Ten). Answering the questions and solving the problems in a workbook may be good fun initially and as a well-spaced variant, but we must consider what may be the effects on a student of knowing that a particular lesson just means a few more pages of the never-ending workbook or that moving from classroom to classroom just means more workbooks? Naturally, the same would apply to the over-use of TV lessons and films, and even of learning games.

The other danger of sameness derives from the fact that all new learning contains an element of stress. Because the learner is initially in a state of not knowing, and cannot be certain that he will succeed in knowing, he is necessarily in a position of uncertainty. Uncertainty contains the threat of failure, that is to say of ineffectiveness. A young child will normally make such cautious and apparently incidental trials at a new task that when he accomplishes it one cannot tell whether he did so by design or chance. However, he will observe the outcome, confirm it by a few more apparently casual trials, and then, as mentioned above, eagerly exploit his new capability for a time. As Berlyne (1960) has demonstrated, too little novelty fails to motivate, but too much is frightening.

Now it may be that a particular method of teaching, or particular teaching materials, have become associated in a child's mind with difficulty and failure. He becomes aversively conditioned to them. If he cannot avoid them physically, such as by staying away from school or the stress-evoking lesson, he will learn a strategy of avoidance within the classroom in the form of a short attention span, daydreaming, or retreating into dullness. As long as the subject is taught by the method that produces the mental block, he will make no progress. If, on the other hand, the teaching of the subject involves the use of a variety of formats, the chances are much greater that the area of avoidance can be circumvented.

9. Is the personal relationship between teacher and students conducive to learning?

This is a difficult subject because notions about what is the correct relationship between teacher and student vary from age to age and culture to culture. Besides securing a good standard of academic attainment, teachers have been expected to transmit the moral attitudes of the culture, to train the younger generation to respect their elders, and to teach them good manners, acceptable personal habits, and a sense of social responsibility. This will no doubt always be part of the job of the teacher, and considering the opportunities for guidance in these respects that the teacher has, it is not unreasonable to ask the teacher to accept such a role.

Nevertheless, the criterion contained in the above question will have to do only with the assessment of the teacher's function in creating good conditions for the learning of the subject matter of instruction. It may be broken down into a number of subcriteria, also put in the form of questions.

1. Is the teacher sufficiently in control of the situation within the classroom to be able to organize and guide the process of learning, and to ensure that the eight conditions listed above are fulfilled? It may not only be that a teacher cannot "keep order." The teacher may be quite happy working informally with any group of children who care to crowd round him or her, and let the remainder of the class do what they like. Or (and how often one sees this), when the teacher decides to inspect the work done, the whole class lines up, and the major part of the lesson is wasted as they stand doing nothing or chewing the corners of their books.

2. Does the teacher believe it is possible to develop the capabilities of the students, or has he/she given way to cynicism, blaming the youngsters, declaring that they are not suitable for the sort of education offered them, etc.? Does the teacher of a special class for the retarded consider it not worthwhile to attempt to teach them any of the basic educational skills because their IQs indicate that they could not master them? If this is the case, the teacher will remain convinced of the low level of mental ability of her class because their capabilities are never tested. Many potentially good teachers become poor teachers because their lack of faith in their ability to teach their students destroys their motivation, and, conversely, a teacher who is performing poorly may often be made to perform well by a restoration of such faith.

3. Does the teacher treat the students with respect and courtesy, or does he/she put down some individuals with sarcastic or other belittling remarks? It is only understandable that students treated in this way will dislike the teacher, and make no effort to do their best for him/her. Likewise, a child openly referred to as the bad boy, or the nuisance of the class, will be tempted to live up to the name. (I would ask teachers to whom the above does not apply not to take it as an imputation on the teaching profession. One has only to visit a number of classes to realize the need for these things to be said.)

4. Does the teacher demonstrate a personal interest in *every* student? The emphasis here is not only on *every* but also on *demonstrate*. A teacher naturally gets more personal gratification from

the good students, and is therefore tempted to call upon them more often to respond, or to use them for taking messages. In a sense a teacher has to be like a politician who never forgets a name and dispenses his smiles and handshakes with studied impartiality. The teacher should make a point of greeting those students who are too shy, indifferent, or hostile to take the initiative in greeting. And in the course of a lesson, as the teacher walks around to look at the students' work, he or she should take the opportunity to demonstrate interest in each individual by whatever means of expressing it comes naturally, whether it be by making an occasional remark or placing a hand on a shoulder, making sure not to overlook those who might feel themselves neglected or out of favor. When every member of a class feels the teacher has a personal interest in him there will be little risk of bad work habits or disorder.

5.   Does the teacher behave with the dignity and authority associated with his/her role? People who have to do the bidding of someone like that person to be superior to them, because it is belittling to take orders from an equal. A teacher who tries to get down to the students' level by using their slang, or "democratically" handing over to them decisions and responsibilities that belong to the role of the teacher, deprives them of an important source of motivation, because they will not work hard to gain the approval of someone whose approval is not worth having.

6.   How does the teacher react towards the badly behaved student? If the teacher sees the bad behavior as a threat to his/her professional competence, the reaction is likely to be one of the alternative responses to threat, either attack or avoidance, and a vicious circle of dislike and antagonism will then develop. Putting a child outside the door or sending him to the principal's office will be interpreted as what it usually is, an act of rejection. This is not to say that a child should never be reported to the principal: there are certain episodes that it is the obvious duty of the teacher to report. Nevertheless, acts of exclusion are to be deprecated as a regular means of discipline because of the aftermath of resentment that they leave. Of course the same applies to physical punishment. A good teacher forestalls the situations that seem to call for these retaliatory measures by establishing a relationship with the class in which they arise only as the outbursts of an extremely dis-

turbed student. A hostile child may commit a provocative act in order to antagonize a teacher and so prevent an affectionate relationship developing. Having been let down previously in his attachments to adults, such a child seeks to defend himself against forming further bonds of affection, which may in turn prove unreliable (see section M of Chapter Ten). A child may also be prone to irrational outbursts as a means of fighting back unbearable memories (see section G of Chapter Ten).

In short, if the teacher has a relationship with the class that makes any general disorder or indiscipline out of the question, the isolated outbreaks may be regarded as signs of individual maladjustment. An indirect but very good way for the teacher to become convinced that this is the case is to complete a checklist of symptoms of disturbed behavior. The realization that the annoying behavior is a form of maladjustment releases the teacher from the feeling of being threatened and substitutes for it a therapeutic responsibility. As one of its authors, I naturally have a preference for the Bristol Social Adjustment Guide, and it has been shown that its mere use by teachers reduces the amount of behavior disturbance (Stott, 1974). In any case, the checklist used should yield a diagnosis that is sufficiently specific to be a guide to treatment. It is not enough to come up with a finding that a badly behaved student has a conduct problem: the teacher knows this already.

It goes without saying that the bad behavior of a whole class cannot be attributed to maladjustment. They may be indulging in an opportunity to arouse emotional reactions in a teacher, and the fun of doing so is more immediate and intense than the milder satisfactions that learning can offer, and in such circumstances the conditions for learning are altogether absent.

The bad behavior of a whole class may also arise from the frustration that comes from aimlessness and boredom. Again, the answer is to ensure that the earlier-stated conditions of learning, i.e., making the process itself rewarding and enjoyable as well as varied, are being met. A deprivation of effectiveness is just as intolerable as physical discomfort. The instinctive response is the same as that to any intolerable situation—either to destroy the offending feature (if one is powerful enough) or to escape from it. The aggressive alternative may take the form of disruptiveness, the escapist one of seeking distractions or just lapsing into a "fed-up" lethargy in which the student expects nothing and gives nothing.

10. Are physical conditions conducive to learning?

It may seem something of an anticlimax to descend from the level of the psychological conditions for learning to the material, but quite elementary material factors are often neglected. The nurseryman who raises houseplants and the householder who wishes to keep them have to maintain a correct temperature, humidity, and light. Human beings also need a controlled environment for proper functioning. The most common physiological insult to which we subject children and teachers in these days, at least on the American continent, is excessive classroom heat. In recent years I have often suffered intense discomfort, and probable befuddlement, from having to work in overheated classrooms. The human brain ceases to function properly if its temperature varies by no more than a degree or so. The loss of behavioral control that excessive temperature may bring about is shown by the increased prevalence of outbreaks of violence during the fetid days of summer in the poorer quarters of American cities, where there is little air conditioning. When children become uncomfortable or are subjected to stress they usually respond by irritability and hyperactivity. Excessive classroom heat may be more worth studying as a cause of the latter condition than the overpublicized danger of food additives. A not infrequent form of impairment among handicapped children is in the mechanisms for maintaining bodily homeostasis. If those for temperature regulation are impaired there is a very real chance that impulsivity and other behavioral impediments to learning may result.

The same applies to excessive noise. Sometimes a handicapped child may be observed putting his hands over his ears at a very moderate noise, as if in pain. These are children in whom the mechanisms for tuning out loud noises are impaired. They may be functioning poorly in anyone who is in a state of fatigue. The constant effort to inhibit noise is stressful even though unconscious. If the effort has to be maintained long enough there is a chance of behavioral breakdown, i.e., avoiding or aggressive action in the form of hyperactivity or irritability. I recently spent part of a morning over some months with a teacher who had a pair of budgerigars in her classroom. Their incessant chattering so got on my nerves that I eventually asked her if she thought it might distract the children. She admitted that it irritated her too, but the birds had been a present from one of the children's parents and she felt awkward about getting rid of them!

I am quite sure that the level of noise produced by the purposeful learning activity of children working together in small groups is neither distracting nor a source of stress. Noises that are attendant upon what one is doing are easily accommodated. Far more serious sources of noise trauma come from the teacher who shouts to make himself heard above a groundswell of chatter, or the frequent puncturing of a classroom environment by much-amplified voices over an intercom system.

SOURCES OF STRESS
FROM OUTSIDE THE LEARNING SITUATION

The sources of stress originating from outside the classroom are too big a subject to be dealt with comprehensively in a discussion of the conditions of learning. It is really a matter of teachers being sensitive to such influences and recognizing it as their duty to refer the children in question to the proper medical, guidance, or social-work agency. If no appropriate agency exists, the school cannot escape the responsibility of raising the matter with the parents. Four areas of neglect that may have to be the subject of counseling are discussed below.

The first of these is malnutrition, of which the typical case in advanced industrial cultures is of the child sent to school without anything to eat owing to the disorganized habits of the parents. Teachers usually become aware of this state of affairs, but all too often fail to initiate remedial action.

The second area of physical neglect comprises untreated, and usually unsuspected, health problems, which may give rise to hyperactivity, lethargy, or mental dullness. Walker's (1975) report on the faults of metabolism and other physical conditions that he has found to cause hyperactivity should be the basis of the medical examination of all chronically restless children. Over-prescription of sedative drugs (often at the insistence of the parents) may produce a learning disablement, as may also chronic intoxication from infected tonsils, adenoids, and ears.

The third area of neglect is lack of sleep, either because of a poorly organized family routine or because of simply staying up to view late-night movies. In an experiment in the remediation of reading difficulties of 8-year-old children, members of the teaching team reported independently of each other that the children in their groups in different schools were bright and alert on Mondays, but good for nothing on Wednesdays. Enquiry revealed that they stayed up late on the Tuesday evenings to watch a television horror serial.

The fourth problem is a source of stress that produces hostility in the child. True hostility (Stott, 1972) is, in my experience, always the reflection of the child's hostile feelings towards his parents, who may nevertheless be affectionate and well-intentioned, but saying and doing things that undermine the child's faith in them (see section M of Chapter Ten).

Any of the above four extra-mural conditions can destroy a child's ability to learn. It is therefore logical for the teacher to be concerned about them, and illogical to spend money and effort in trying to teach children suffering from such handicaps without at the same time putting into motion such remedial resources as are available.

CHAPTER NINE

The Learning Environment and The Teacher Variable

*If I am to listen to the opinion of another person
it must be expressed positively.
Of things problematical
I have enough in myself.*
J. W. Goethe

MATCHING TEACHING STYLES AND CHILDREN

It is coming to be recognized that the most important part of the student's learning environment is that part provided by the teacher. This simple truth has stimulated thought about the matching of the teaching style to the learning needs of the individual child (Hunt, 1971). Hunt recommends that teachers should be trained to develop a repertoire of styles that could be matched to each child's needs. Such flexibility, if it can be attained, would of course be admirable. The difficulty would be in training teachers in such versatility. Actors are selected for their flair for putting themselves in different roles, but teachers are not. The mastery of a repertoire of roles would require intensive training, since it is notoriously hard for anyone, including the student teacher, to apply rules that have been derived from academic analysis.

More important, training of the teacher to play varied roles seems to imply that the business of teaching and learning should center on the teacher. The teacher's function should be to provide good conditions for learning and to organize the process of learning in every student's mind. When the teacher becomes more an organizer and stimulator than a performer/role-player, the limitations to flexibility that the teacher's personality imposes become less decisive. Rather than the teacher's playing different roles, we ought to think of providing each child with his appropriate niche, in which the conditions of learning are as nearly optimal for him as possible. It is hard to conceive how this could be achieved so long as the range of environments is limited to those in which the teacher is generating the action and the pupils are the recipients, because experience shows us that this in itself is an unacceptable role for many children. In short, the teacher has got to step off the center of the stage. The teaching space would then be a setting for a number of learning activities, some carried out in groups, and some individual. The flexibility needed to provide each child with the appropriate learning niche would be inherent in such a situation. For each child the teacher could check whether the ten conditions of learning set out above are being met, and, if any are not, consider how the necessary adjustments may be made. In this way the teacher's function becomes an objective skill that is independent of the needs or limitations of his or her own personality.

It is common nowadays to hear pessimistic views expressed about the poor quality of teaching (hence that cynical word "dys-teachia"), and of the need for a radical overhaul of teacher education, so that, as it were, we can make a fresh start. However, pious exhortations to raise standards of teaching, and complaints about low standards, will have little effect without an analysis of the reasons for our present shortcomings. It is overlooked that teachers can suffer just as much as their pupils from the progressive deterioration that comes of frustration and discouragement. A former colleague of mine who voiced such pessimism also once made an observation that seems to me to provide the answer. It was that some teachers whom she had regarded as "hopeless" became enthusiastic and effective once they had been shown techniques that worked; they had responded to the reinforcement of success. In a sense this is retraining, but it is by a method of demonstration at a very practical level. Everything depends upon our possession of a science of pedagogy based on the study of the conditions for effective learning.

It goes without saying that in the long-term the application of such a lore to the classroom is a matter of a more systematic training of teachers in professional skills analogous to the training of a doctor, dentist, or engineer. In the meantime, for the benefit of the next generation of students, we shall need a profession of specialists whose function will be to train and advise teachers as to the sort of learning environment they provide. As has been seen, because the above criteria are based in part upon the psychology of learning, it would be logical for the school psychologist to have a share in such a service. However, because the criteria were also based in part upon teaching experience, it would also be necessary to involve specialists with a considerable and successful teaching record. We would therefore hope for an alliance between the psychological and curriculum services of an education authority, in order to foster the optimal conditions of learning possible in the light of our present resources and knowledge.

DEALING WITH MISMATCHES

No doubt we shall have to wait many years before the science of pedagogy is so advanced, and generally applied, that every child is provided with an optimal learning environment. For a long time yet, therefore, we shall have to deal with breakdowns of individual teacher/pupil relations.

Such "mismatches" are usually seen in terms of a personality clash between teacher and child, with the pragmatic solution being placement of the child with another teacher. This presupposes that there is a teacher of a parallel class with whom the child would be happier, or that the child can be moved to a neighboring school. Such a step may be necessary as a crisis measure, but it obviously cannot be a solution to every case, and there is a danger of the child who is a misfit everywhere being shuttled around from school to school.

To explain a breakdown in a teacher-student relationship as a personality clash may also block helpful diagnosis of the cause of the trouble, i.e., we may fasten upon a rather superficial verbal formulation that absolves us from exploring the issue further. Nevertheless, personality clashes in the classroom have to be explored. If a teacher clashes with one child now and then, there is a possibility that he or she is providing an adverse learning environment for many other children that reaches a crisis only once in a while. Alternatively, the child may be suffering from a type of behavior disturbance that requires urgent attention and that may be misinterpreted and mishandled without help. The "misfit" in these cases can arise from a vicious circle of deteriorating relationships.

Because the mishandling of the situation may not be obvious, expert professional help may be needed. Too open an offer of friendship to an extremely hostile child may provoke bad behavior as a means of maintaining the hostility. When this happens, the emotionally hurt teacher feels let down and decides the child is a bad egg. However, the teacher who understands the mechanisms of hostility need not let things go so far. A personality clash would be an indication that the teacher has no such insight into the state of the hostile child, and so reacts subjectively (as I have known principals of training schools for delinquents to do). In short, the occurrence of a personality clash should not be dealt with merely by separating the clashers, but should be seen as a danger signal of some more general cause of concern.

Each misfit (or personality clash) between teacher and student should be diagnosed with the same care that is given to the causes of a street accident. The methodology of such diagnosis will need to be refined, along with the training of specialist advisers and the building-up of a case literature from which experiences could be brought together in a body of professional practice.

Such guidelines for the diagnosis of misfits as I can here offer perforce draw upon only a limited range of professional experience and lack a comprehensive body of case literature. If I were asked to investigate a crisis of this nature I would first try to understand the teacher's style of teaching and of handling a class. In the review given in Chapter Seven, of the children referred, quite a few were cases where the mismatch could be diagnosed as arising from a failure of teaching method. A child whose logical mind and strong need for effectiveness demanded a systematic phonic approach to reading was impatient with the sight method (language experience) used in the class. A first grade boy who was a good reader resented having to complete pages of letters in a workbook; he was isolated behind a screen and denied suitable reading materials (the teacher even withheld the books I brought in for him). It is in such cases that the vicious circle of bad attitudes and learning blocks develops. This part of my diagnosis would therefore consist in a systematic review of the learning environment to see if any of the conditions for good learning are absent.

The next step would be to obtain a description of the child's behavior and attitudes in school by asking the teacher to complete a checklist. The teacher would not be asked for opinions or interpretations, except in so far as people can be relied upon to describe other people's attitudes and moods (Stott, 1974). Such observations must be taken strictly for what they are, namely a record of how the child reacts to a given situation. They may reflect his type of temperament or his way of responding to particular stresses.

The third stage in the diagnosis would be to hear from the parents about the child's life at home: his health and development, whether he plays constructively and with good concentration and initiative, how he gets on with other children, what difficulties his parents may have with him, and what their expectations are about his progress in school. Comparison of his mode of coping at home with that within the school would help me to judge whether his inability to get on with his teacher was more a matter of a general maladjustment or a particular reaction to the kind of situation that the teacher was providing for him.

A recommendation for removal to another class (if this is feasible) would be made only if 1) the cause of the clash is judged to be the teacher's way of teaching and there seems little chance of modifying it, or 2) the child's general maladjustment is such that it cannot be handled within the regular classroom.

A CASE HISTORY

The case of 8-year-old Jimmy illustrates the need for the systematic diagnosis of mismatching. Jimmy had been brought by his parents to the Center for Educational Disabilities because his class teacher made complaints about his lack of progress, had had him placed in a remedial reading group, and foresaw that he would have to repeat Grade 3. These reports greatly surprised the parents because Jimmy was an ardent reader at home, often spending hours reading in his room (the usual craze of an 8-year-old who discovers the joys of reading). He was also placed in a remedial mathematics group, although at home he would happily spend over an hour doing mathematics on his father's calculator. He enjoyed playing card games, and was quite proficient at a number of them (an indication of normal perceptual ability and powers of concentration). Moreover, he was keenly interested in anything mechanical and was very good at carrying out art projects, even those involving photography, with the help of his father.

At home Jimmy had never been a disciplinary problem. He was a good mixer and was kind to other children, especially his three younger sisters. The only criticism his parents made of him was that he was a non-conformist: he liked to do things his own way, and if he couldn't he got bored.

His teacher's account of him could have been that of quite a different boy. She said he would not complete his work, and when he had to take it home he delayed bringing it in or lost it. His writing was spread in a disorganzied fashion all over the page. He would not work on his own or follow instructions, either those given to him personally or those given to him as a member of a group. His attainment was inconsistent: sometimes he understood, sometimes he didn't; his test results were either near-perfect or a dismal failure. Mostly he was apathetic and given to daydreaming. From his performance on the Frostig the teacher had diagnosed a perceptual-motor problem.

The psychologist visited the school in an effort to resolve the contradiction between Jimmy-at-home and Jimmy-at-school. She found a very well-organized classroom, with desks in straight, perfect rows. Every child had to set out the day's work in the same way. Repeatedly in the course of an explanation the teacher would pause and say "Got it, Jimmy?" After the class had done a test she went over to him and picked up his paper, saying, "Jimmy is the only one who doesn't follow instructions." The teacher was amazed at a project that he had done in the Center, and voiced the suspicion that he had not done it on his own.

Among the behavioral descriptions of Jimmy marked by the teacher on the Bristol Social Adjustment Guide were:

General manner with teacher:	Quite cut off from people, you can't get near him as a person.
Asking teacher's help:	Too lacking in energy to bother.
Paying attention in class:	You can't get his attention.
Working by himself:	Unmotivated, has no energy.
Facing new learning tasks:	Has not the confidence to try anything difficult.

The above description characterized Jimmy as a maladjusted child with five indications of unforthcomingness, four of withdrawal, six of depression, and four other, more generalized symptoms of underreaction. In the Center he showed himself to be a talented child who was very forthcoming in displaying his knowledge. He was eager to try anything new and to tackle difficult words. He asked questions, was forward in conversation, and entered into any game with a boyish competitive zest. However—and this was the thread of similarity that ran through his behavior in every situation—he wanted to be in control and do things his own way. In a test he ignored the instructions and went ahead and started it on his own. Far from being withdrawn and timid, he was an irrepressible little fellow.

His poor performance in class was understandable. With his high effectiveness-motivation, taking the form of an insistence on dealing with his environment creatively and in an independent manner—to the extent of breaking the rules and refusing to follow the behests of the teacher—he found himself at the mercy of a teacher who insisted upon a complete conformity to rule and procedure. Powerless as he was to do anything else (an 8-year-old can still be physically overawed by an adult) he responded in part by a stonewalling withdrawal and in part by retreating into the world of his dreams. A creative child had been made into a slow learner.

It is of interest to count how many of the conditions for a good learning environment described and numbered in the preceding chapter were denied to this boy. He was certainly deprived of enjoyment (No. 1), since the process of learning was neither absorbing, rewarding, nor enjoyable to him. The same applied to No. 4 (working at his own pace), since he was forced to advance at a uniform rate of progress with the rest of the class and was denied any opportunity to exercise his talents. With regard to No. 5 (learning by his own mental activity), he was a boy who was learning fast by his own mental activity, but not in the classroom. The classroom set-up precluded any learning within a peer-group (No. 6), and indeed such a method was far from his teacher's mind. The uniform rate of progress imposed by the teacher was monotonous to a boy with his active mind (No. 8: Are the learning situations varied?). Finally, and above all, being continually harried and shown up by the teacher was not the sort of personal relationship between teacher and student that was conducive to learning (No. 9). In short, six of the conditions for good learning were denied him, and because of this deprivation the others became inapplicable.

In the case of Jimmy, mere removal to another class would not have been sufficient. The chances are that he had already developed mental strategies for tuning out, and his insistence on doing his own thing could run him into trouble with another teacher. To counter the bad learning style he had fallen into, he would need a period of encouragement and freedom to develop his talent for creative projects.

One is also led to wonder how many other Jimmys have been or are going to be made into slow learners by similar insensitivity of handling. The independent, non-conforming child will be able to apply his creativity in socially useful ways only if he has the basic education to enable him to operate at a high level. In default of this he will be forced into socially unacceptable forms of enterprise. In terms of cost-benefit, the identification and correct nurturing of children of this type would give a large pay-off to a nation that is in dire need of people who are both creative and educated.

CHAPTER TEN

Guidelines for Teachers in The Remediation of Faulty Learning Styles

Let us first turn to the experiences of Charles Darwin.
I want you to visualize not the great naturalist of the middle of the 19th century,
but a boy of 22 who had unsuccessfully started to train as a doctor,
then as a parson, who had just taken an undistinguished pass degree at Cambridge
and, through the good offices of his professor of botany,
had been offered an unpaid job.
Most of us could manage as good a record as that.
But Darwin was an ardent collector of beetles . . .
. . . he was a keen amateur geologist.
Dame Helen Gwynne-Vaughan

Alongside the compilation of the *Guide to the Child's Learning Skills* (GCLS), a number of remedial devices designed to correct the faulty learning behaviors observed were developed. The methodology anticipated the procedures of a formative evaluation outlined by Guralnick (1973). The evaluation entailed the experimental use of each remedial item with a succession of children, modifying it to correct defects or to extend its range to different varieties of educational handicaps. The identification of the latter in behavioral terms by means of the GCLS gives definition to the faults in learning style that are the main target of the remediation.

These Guidelines offer suggestions for the correction of the faults of learning style identified. They recommend, first, the appropriate remedial materials, and second, the kind of relationship the teacher should maintain with the child. Directions for the standard methods of use of the materials are not given, since these are contained in the manuals to the Flying Start Kits (Stott, 1971).

It will be found that the teacher will nearly always mark more than one type of faulty learning behavior for each educationally high-risk child. The reason for this is that behavioral handicaps to learning may be either primary, in the sense that they are the original causes of the failure to learn, or secondary, in the sense that they are reactions to the failure produced by the original handicap. Among the most frequent of the original causes are types of temperament or behavior disturbance (i.e., readinesses to behave in certain ways) that are not conducive to learning. Examples are unforthcomingness, impulsivity, hostility, and depression. Among the original causes must also be reckoned environmental influences, such as those that go with social disadvantage and adverse educational experiences, and also physical handicaps and chronic health conditions.

To the extent that these original causes result in the child's falling behind and getting bewildered and discouraged, they prompt him to react either by avoiding the challenges of learning or by compensating for the position of ineffectiveness and inferiority in which he finds himself. The particular strategies of avoidance or compensation to which he resorts will be decided by his temperament and the lifestyle of his community. The unforthcoming child will be tempted to play dull or even to retreat into retardation, the impulsive child to seek and create distractions. Consequently, it is usual to find that a characteristic group of faulty learning styles will be marked for a child who is experiencing learning difficulties, and they will both reflect the original causes and represent the child's attempts to defend himself against failure (which only make the failure worse).

General prescriptions handed out by psychologists have proved ineffective because teachers need guidance in the detailed remedial procedures to be followed with each child. Nevertheless, because different types of temperament and of reaction to failure can be recognized, it is possible to classify faulty approaches to learning and to suggest ways of correcting them that have proved effective with similar children. This is what these Guidelines set out

to do. The capital letters in parentheses refer to the sections of the
GCLS, with the section headings, also in capitals, reproduced for
the convenience of the reader.

(A) HE/SHE IS AFRAID TO BEGIN
OR TO COMMIT HIMSELF TO AN ANSWER

This section describes the apprehensiveness of the unforthcoming
child in a learning situation.

What prevents a child of this sort from applying his mind to
the solving of problems is his assumption of, and fear of, failure. We
therefore set out to condition him to adopt an attitude of "I can do
it." We give him exceedingly easy tasks, which he will be able to
solve immediately once he agrees to try or even to look at the
materials. Examples are the *Two-Piece Puzzles*.

The unforthcoming child should never be left in a position of
stalling and bewilderment, since this will confirm his conviction
that the problem is beyond him. On the other hand, we should
never do the task for him, because this reinforces the strategy often
adopted by such children of getting the adult to provide the answers. In the event of stalling, the teacher should make the task
easier, but the final solution must always come from the child. It
may be necessary, for example, to move the two halves of the picture close together so that they are almost touching. When the child
completes the picture by joining the halves, he is praised.

Having engineered one act of successful participation, the
teacher should provide more activities at the same level of difficulty. We have to resist the temptation, in our elation at having got
a correct response, to rush the child on to something harder. He
needs a period of easy and certain success for the "I can do it"
conditioning to take place.

With the unforthcoming child it is equally important to know
what not to do. Merely having to answer to an adult may be too
frightening to such a child, and may throw him into a state of
confusion that will reinforce his retreat into non-participation. Instead of conditioning him to expect success we would be conditioning him to use dullness as a defense. Children who have developed
this strategy naturally get very low IQ scores, and every school for
the retarded contains some children like this. We know nothing
about their mental abilities until we can get them to use their
minds.

The unforthcoming child learns best in his own time, by what Bruner (1966) calls observational learning. Group games provide a setting in which this can take place: examples are learning the letter-sound associations with the *Things Alive Cards* or the *Giant Touch Cards* of the Programmed Reading Kit (Stott, 1962). The child can observe other children's choices in silence, then, when he is sure of himself, he will break in.

(B) BRIGHT OR DULL AS IT PLEASES HIM TO BE

The key portion of the descriptions in this section is that the child's dullness is not consistent in every aspect of his life. Children have all sorts of reasons for adopting a defense of dullness—to which our readiness to account for failure in terms of "low intelligence" makes us easy victims. Children from deep rural backgrounds and from certain ethnic minority groups can be adept at stonewalling against the dominant culture. It is a skill handed down to them through the generations. Children with an excessive need for dependence often find that they can use a pose of retardation to good effect. Those, like Down's-syndrome children, who have been accorded the role of retardates, very often become clever at exploiting it for their own convenience. If their behavior is subjected to the test of "Who gains?" it becomes apparent that very few retarded children are as dull as their performance indicates. There are children who compensate for failure by doing things deliberately wrong, just to show they don't care. Perhaps the most exasperating and difficult to deal with are those who enjoy the personal attention they get in a remedial situation and maintain a front of dullness to make sure that they never graduate from it.

The key to the planning of a remedial program for these pseudo-dullards or pseudo-retardates is to bear in mind that their defenses are against *adult* pressures. In a game with their age-peers they lose face by pretending to be stupid. For example, in the posting game of the *Mail Boxes* there is no fun in being told time after time that one is wrong when, with a moment's attention, one can be right. The certainty with which success can be obtained in this game, by using only a modicum of concentration, makes it almost embarrassingly popular with young children, to the extent that teachers have sometimes used it as a reward for a period of work at some other task.

How do we deal with children who play dull in order to be able to command individual attention? We cannot simply refuse them help, yet in helping them we risk reinforcing their strategy. Our tactic has been to say something like, "See if you can make pictures with these cards" (giving the child something well within his capability, such as the *Four-Piece Puzzles*), "I'll come back when you've done two." The teacher then walks away and helps another child or group, meanwhile watching what is happening out of the corner of his eye. As soon as the child has completed the task, the teacher approaches again and, if the child has done it correctly, gives praise and spends a little time with the child. If the task has been done incorrectly, the teacher quickly walks away again with the light-hearted remark, "I think you're trying to do it wrong." In this way, the child gets attention by being clever rather than by being stupid.

Often it is effective to call the bluff of the pseudo-dullard in a joking sort of way, such as by saying, "I think you're just teasing me. You are doing it wrong purposely to see if I'll notice." The child can then give up his pretense without losing face. (This tactic succeeded with the very unforthcoming Barbara, whose deliberate mistakes can be seen in the film "Learning to Learn." In "Johnny Can Learn to Read," filmed a year later, she can be seen taking obvious pleasure in getting correct answers.)

With culturally transmitted pseudo-dullness one would obviously not use such tactics. With these children it is a matter of never trying to hurry them, but rather putting them in a game situation in which caution and making sure bring success, and where they have plenty of time to learn from observing what other children do.

(C) HE/SHE HAS SOLITARY, PECULIAR WAYS OF USING LEARNING OR PLAY MATERIALS

In this category fall widely varying sorts of withdrawn children, from those with autistic tendencies to the elective mute. They require highly specialized clinical treatment that is beyond the scope of these notes. Nevertheless, the remedial teacher can be of some help in exploring the capabilities of such children and their willingness to get involved in learning activities. The Flying Start program has certain advantages in this respect in that it does not require the child to speak, and the activities can be carried out by a child playing by himself. On the other hand they provide opportunities for the withdrawn child to learn to interact with an adult or another child. One advantage of a highly structured program of learning activities is that the therapist can record a rate of progress that is slow by normal learning standards, and hence may be hardly discernible to someone relying on memory of what the child was like three or six months back. The Progress Cards of the Flying Start Program record not only achievement but also the rate of improvement in deployment of learning skills. In addition, there is available for clinical and research use a more detailed recording booklet[1] in which each response of the child can be entered.

(D) HE/SHE ACTS WITHOUT TAKING TIME
TO LOOK OR TO WORK THINGS OUT

So-called hyperactive behavior takes so many different forms, and has so many different origins, that the term has limited diagnostic value. Because we need to identify the actual behaviors that are interfering with the child's learning, the term "hyperactive" is not used in the GCLS.

Section D isolates a basic fault of learning behavior, which consists of not allowing time for the focusing of attention or for information to be processed through the mind. The impulsivity of children displaying this learning style is such that their perceptual and mental abilities are hardly used, and hence are inadequately developed. Those most seriously affected become retardates, and they are well represented in schools for the retarded. Any attempt to assess their mental ability is futile because they will no more use their eyes and ears or reflect upon a problem in an intelligence test than they will in a learning situation.

Our remedial strategy with these children is to place before them some very attractive activity in which they can succeed with only a little attention. The posting of the Mail Box cards has this sort of appeal. If the poster doesn't check the letter on his card against the letter on the box, his partner is likely to pronounce him wrong. This pulls him up with a jolt, and in nearly all cases one observes an immediate change in the child's tactics: he moves his card carefully along the row of letters on the boxes until he has found the right one. He had learned the strategy required for success. In a few moments his impulsivity has been mastered: for its cure he will need similar experiences in a number of activities, so that the conditioning can be generalized into a good learning habit of attentiveness and taking the time to think out an answer.

---

[1]*Developing the Child's Potentiality*, available from D. H. Stott, 30 Colborn Street, Guelph, Ontario, Canada, NIG 2M5. The price is $2.00 per copy, and permission to reprint the booklet is included.

Several additional Flying Start activities, described in Appendix B, were designed to condition the impulsive child to take time to think out his responses. The *Merry-Go-Rounds* place him in a game situation in which he has to learn to cooperate and to await his turn. The *Animal Puzzles* demonstrate the advantages of a methodical strategy. The *Matchers* make success conditional upon noting three criteria before making a choice.

The degree of success these conditioning procedures have depends upon the source of the disorganized behavior. Some children have never been in a situation where attention and calm thought brought rewards. Their only idea of fun is romping and rough play, and their strategy for getting what they want is to grab while it's there. This sort of educationally high-risk child, from a disadvantaged environment, usually adapts himself to a good learning style very quickly: he has the perceptual and mental capacity but it has been lying dormant.

Where the impulsivity and lack of attentional focus are caused by neurological dysfunction, we must of course expect a slower response to the conditioning, and in a few cases it is very slow indeed. The important thing is that, prior to the child's exposure to the program, it is difficult to distinguish environmental from neurological impulsivity. Even those children who suffer from a neurological dysfunction may respond to some extent. Except in the most extreme cases, their difficulty in controlling and organizing their learning behavior is relative, depending upon how attractive the activities are to them and the extent to which they can attain and enjoy success. The conditioning process may have to be continued with great patience over a long time, but the final result will be more permanent than treatment by drugs because the child is learning to control his impulsivity in natural, real-life activities.

(E) HE/SHE IS EASILY DISTRACTED

Distractibility, in the sense of lack of perseverance at a task, can also have very different origins. There is no doubt that an inability to exclude irrelevant stimuli can be caused by damage or dysfunction of the higher brain mechanisms. On the other hand, distractibility can be a form of avoidance used as a defense against confusion and failure. The reasons for the latter may lie outside the child: for example, frequent changes of school during the early years, or lack of home training in fine attention or concentration. Just as the temperamentally apprehensive child uses an assumed dullness as an avoidance strategy, so the temperamentally active and impulsive child will resort to enterprising tricks for evading the distasteful situation. I am against shielding distractible children from possible distractions. They have to learn to concentrate under normal classroom conditions. The positive approach is to tempt them with activities that offer them a clearly visible goal, which, however, requires a little concentration time to attain. It is also an advantage if the activities are of such a nature that they can be resumed after occasional interruptions. For younger children there is the Noah's Ark game with the *Left-Right Cards*. The animals are placed to the left or right of the gangway according to which way they face. As the activity progresses they form impressively long lines across the classroom. The placing of the animals entails a certain amount of physical movement, which makes the activity more congenial to these children. Older children can play "Concentration" (finding the pairs of similar animals from the cards laid out face downwards), which is an excellent training, as the name implies.

Second, there are the *Families Cards,* consisting of sets of six pictures depicting objects within the same category, such as eating utensils, garments, furniture, vehicles, animals, and pairs of letters and numerals. There are many games involving the collecting of sets that can be played with these cards, but quite a good tactic is simply to throw a heap of the cards on a table or floor and invite the children to play with them. They will very soon realize the possibility of making up sets. None of these activities, consisting in arranging cards, is spoilt by occasional distractibility, because the sets remain in position pending resumption of the activity, and an unfinished set is a challenge to completion. We find that children will remain absorbed in playing with the Families cards for a surprisingly long time.

(F) HE/SHE IS OVER-ACTIVE AND FIDGETY

This section includes those children who distract themselves from their learning by constant movement of the limbs, swinging on their chair (and sometimes slipping off it or falling over backwards), or getting up and running around. In extreme cases such "hyperactivity" can be the result of brain dysfunction or damage, but it is unwise to come to this conclusion until every resource of training has been tried. The child may never have had access to activities that reward quiet concentration, and consequently may have developed "hyperactivity" as a style of life. It is extremely difficult to diagnose the nature of the fidgetiness until the child is introduced to activities in which he wants so much to concentrate, in order to succeed, that he keeps still of his own accord, even though only momentarily at first. Any simple table game with an adult should provide such a situation.

There are some children neurologically constituted in such a way that they find keeping still uncomfortable, like a smoker deprived of nicotine sedation. One of the boys (Glenn) in the Flying Start documentary film "Learning to Learn" was of this type. His mother, who worked as a volunteer in our Center at Guelph, taught him to concentrate by telling him he would be able to pick the right card if he kept his feet still. He had only to do so for a moment, but this gave him freedom from the distraction of fidgeting for enough time to make a correct choice. Concentrating on keeping his feet still served as a ritual that enabled him to overcome his fidgetiness, and he became a good learner. His faith in the ritual was such that once, when his mother made an intentional mistake to encourage him, he exclaimed "Mummy, keep your feet still."

Almost any simple, quiet activity can afford a training in overcoming physical restlessness, provided the child enters into the spirit of the game and is motivated to do well. Only with such motivation are we able to assess the possibilities of cure or control.

(G) HE/SHE CAN AT TIMES HAVE UNPREDICTABLE OUTBURSTS

The unprovoked outbursts of these children are often of an alarming character that may be interpreted as psychotic episodes. From well-authenticated cases at the Guelph Center we were able to see them as the means by which the affected child tried to blot out the memory of some distressing aspect of his family life. In short, they are avoidance gestures of the same type as the displacement activities that Lorenz and Tinbergen observed in animals, but of a more violent and drastic nature. They consequently indicate the need for a social-work investigation of the child's family circumstances. The effect of the outbursts in school is often to exasperate and antagonize the teacher, which in turn generates hostility in the child. Needless to say, such children need cool, sympathetic handling. One such child, whose father made violent attacks on his mother, in the early part of his time at the Center would suddenly fly at the teacher and bite her. At other times he would sweep the learning materials off the table. These outbursts occurred without warning or provocation, just when something reminded him of the danger that his mother was in from his father.

The telltale feature of this type of behavior disorder, which distinquishes it from the various forms of hyperactivity, is that, when there is no reminder of the distressing home circumstances or traumatic event, the child will normally behave calmly, show good concentration, and be a good learner.

The social-work treatment of the family situation is outside the scope of these notes. However, within the remedial setting advantage can be taken of the child's good learning potential (unless of course he is affected by some handicap of temperament in addition). The essence of the remedial treatment is to establish a good personal relationship with the child, so that he is prepared to accept an intensive and challenging learning program. This will serve to keep his mind occupied, and so render the distressing reminders of his home worries less frequent, meanwhile preventing the bad relationships that his outbursts create from degenerating into a general attitude of antagonism. [With older boys, the need to find some means of suppressing the distressing memories often induces them to seek out excitements that may take a delinquent form (Stott, 1950).]

(H)   HE/SHE LOOKS FOR WAYS OF EVADING LEARNING TASKS

This section describes the typical avoiding attitude of the child with an outgoing, active temperament. The aversive feelings that they have built up against learning tasks, or any activity needing thought, are described by them as tiredness. They find that complaints of being tired are hard for the adult to resist, the teacher being naturally aware of the danger of exercising pressure. The truth is that children who are really tired seldom say they are; they just relapse into lethargy or irritability. The telltale indication is whether the child is listless in his play. If he comes to life outside the classroom, his "tiredness" may be interpreted as an avoidance strategy. To accept the excuse at its face value is to demonstrate its efficacy and hence reinforce it. We have found that the best way to counter refusals to continue that are obviously manifestations of avoidance-tiredness is to ask the child if he would like to choose another of the learning activities. This offer is nearly always accepted as a compromise, and the teacher should fall in with the choice even though it may be much below the level of the child's capabilities. If the offer is not accepted, the teacher may say, "Well, if you're tired, perhaps you would like to sit and rest awhile." The child should not be allowed to wander about the room, but the materials should be left for him to come back to in his own time, or, better still, a group-game might be organized which he is free to join. In an attractive group activity, complaints of being tired are seldom heard.

(J) HE/SHE SETS ABOUT TASKS AS IF HE DOESN'T CARE

The lack of motivation described in this section can have various origins and be of varying depth. Usually, after a short period of reluctance to get involved, the appeal of a learning game will draw the child in. Boys from a disadvantaged background with an aggressive lifestyle may voice blustering refusal to do any work. With such a group in our Guelph Center we instituted a behavior-modification program, the reward in which was a 10-minute spell of play at a table-hockey game. Each period of good work, lasting between 10 and 20 minutes according to the stage in the program, earned three points. Nine points were needed for a ticket entitling its holder to 10 minutes of play on the hockey board. In order to avoid disappointment and to make it more worthwhile to work and behave well in the next session, a student who earned less than the requisite nine points in one session was allowed to carry them over to the next. The points were recorded by markers in a peg board, so that the progress of each student towards the full complement of nine was always visible. Eventually one of the group said to the teacher, "Look here, why bother about all these points? We'll work well and you just give us our hockey tickets."

Some children with a highly developed need for effectiveness compensate for failure by putting on a front of not caring, and even taking a perverse pride in giving wrong answers. Usually they are dominant children who like taking the lead. The obvious ploy is to put them in the leadership position in a game such as *Things Alive* or the Dice in *Learning about Number*.

(K) HE/SHE SUFFERS
AT TIMES (OR CONSTANTLY) FROM A LACK OF ENERGY

This section describes a lack of motivation of a depressed type. When it is observed in a young child the first thing to investigate is a possible health problem—infected tonsils, adenoids, or ears and glandular imbalance are the chief culprits. During the middle years it may be a matter of lack of sleep because of late-night movies or a disorganized family life, to which may be added malnutrition. Chronic depression coupled with irritable outbursts may also be the result of long-standing family stresses. Lifelessness is not natural in children, and when seen it should be the subject of medical and social-work investigation until the reasons for it come to light.

(L) HE/SHE RELIES ON PERSONAL CHARM TO AVOID LEARNING

During my work with delinquent youths, I noted that very few of them were physically attractive: the exceptions were the really hardened rogues. An attractive youth has to be exceptionally wayward to alienate the readiness of teachers, social workers, and judges to make allowances for him.

The child who uses natural charm to avoid learning has similar advantages. Everyone (or nearly so) is conned. In the Guelph Center we have had more than one charming little girl referred who exploited pattern B ("dull or bright as it pleases him to be"). Indeed, playing dull in order to command individual attention is all the more effective if the teacher can be reinforced by the exercise of charm. In a boy the reinforcement may not only be good looks and a winning smile; it can be perfect manners, studied helpfulness, elegant conversation—all the arts of the courtier.

The beginning of remediation with these charmers is to realize what is happening (which is harder than it may sound from the above). It is then a matter of planning counter-measures to ensure that the "charmers" are never accorded privileged duties that take them away from learning tasks and of requiring that a reasonable time be spent on learning activities. If playing dull is also suspected, the remedial tactics suggested above under section B apply. That is to say, the teacher, being aware of the instinctive appeals that the child is using, is careful to respond only to good learning behavior, and if possible to place the child in a group-learning situation with his age-peers, who will be less easily seduced by charm than an adult.

(M) HE/SHE HAS HOSTILE MOODS DURING WHICH HE REFUSES TO WORK

True hostility, as a form of behavior disturbance, must be distinguished from antagonism (which may have a cultural or social origin) and from aggressiveness (which may be an expression of personal dominance unaccompanied by bad feeling). In the state of hostility the child repels friendly overtures and puts up a defense against the establishment of them in the form of sullenness (to be distinguished from sulking about not getting his own way). In addition, the hostile child often commits provocative acts of disobedience and deviance which he reckons will arouse anger, his purpose being in effect to invite rejection.

Hostility originates in the child's loss of faith in the loyalty of his parents. Having become convinced by their threats to "put him away," hand him over to the officers of the law, or by the threat of one parent or the other to desert the home and thus abandon him, the child responds by setting out to break the relationship once and for all. The hostility generated thus becomes a self-banishing reaction and an attempt to kill undependable love by hate. It is analogous to the rage of the jilted lover, which has a biological advantage in that the spurned one can start afresh with a more promising partner. Like all moods, hostility tends to transfer itself from one person to another, and the teacher gets the brunt of an emotional disturbance that the child brings to school with him.

Because the cause of the child's hostility lies in the family relationships, its remediation is properly the responsibility of the psychologist or social worker. The parents should be counseled against uttering threats that could be interpreted as rejection or talking about desertion in front of the child. If they follow this course and do nothing else to undermine the child's security, the hostility will cease (Stott, 1972, Chapter 6). Because children have a fundamental need for permanent family attachments, they will put up with virtually anything not to jeopardize those they have, with only their loss of confidence in such ties inducing them to react by relation-breaking hostility. Once the parents desist from threats and behavior that undermines his faith in them, the child does his best to reestablish himself in his family; the hostility is replaced by an anxiety to please and be helpful. If no psychological or social agency is available, the teacher or principal may have to undertake this family counseling, since little educational progress will be made with the child as long as his hostility persists.

Apart from guidance to the parents, the teacher can do a great deal to mitigate the hostility by not meeting the child's expectation of rejection. Once the motivation of the sullenness and deviant behavior is recognized, the teacher no longer feels personally threatened by the disciplinary breaches, or compelled to mete out regular punishment. There is no danger that the class as a whole will get out of hand if the teacher accords special treatment to the hostile child. He will be unpopular with his classmates, and far from modeling their behavior on him they will dissociate themselves from what they regard as foolishness. The teacher must in effect refuse to be provoked by the hostile child's attempts to secure rejection. Hostility that fails to produce a bad relationship loses its point, and the child may begin to have second thoughts. Nevertheless, too open an offer of friendship will be met by an emotionally highly-charged rejection, and, possibly, by running out of the classroom. Angry refusal to work or quitting the group should be met by studied coolness, and a suggestion that the child might like to sit by himself somewhere. The child should then be allowed to sit out his sullenness or hostility, and be accepted unobtrusively into the group when he wishes to return. At the first opportunity a comment might be made upon something he has done well. If a child persists in his hostile mood nothing is gained by trying to cajole him out of it. However, a really bad day is often followed by a good one; the exercise of patience and kind consideration have had a delayed-action effect, and hostility can be replaced by urgent bids for approval and affection. So long as the child remains hostile he will do poorly at his work because he seeks disapproval rather than approval. As he learns to value the teacher's interest in him he will develop an incentive to do his best.

(N) HE/SHE SEEMS TO TRY TO ATTEND, AND IS NOT HYPERACTIVE OR DISTRACTIBLE, BUT CANNOT CONCENTRATE

Nearly always, "short attention span" is due to a conditioned distaste for the material to be learned owing to previous experience of failure. When the child seems unable to keep his mind on his work to the extent that he gives silly answers to questions that a short while ago he got right, we have to suspect the operation of such an avoidance mechanism. The subject matter of the learning has become so much associated with failure, pressure, and possibly ridicule or harsh treatment at his failure that—try as he may—he cannot keep his mind on it. The avoidance is a flight of his mind from the topic, which, with his present anxieties, he cannot control.

Obviously, making learning still more distasteful by trying to force concentration will only render the avoidance more pathological. Traditional one-to-one tuition, which involves cornering the child into providing answers, may have that effect. If the avoidance conditioning is to be overcome, the learning situation must be happy and free of pressure. It may be necessary first to develop a liking for table games and puzzles that have little formal learning content, and subsequently to introduce those that lead to a structured learning program. Once the child has mastered the rudiments and has gained confidence in his learning ability there will be no rationale for the avoidance, alias short attention span, and it will cease to be a problem.

This conditioned short attention span should be distinguished from a characteristic *fading out* of concentration. The child concentrates well for a few moments and gets his answers right. Then his mind peters out like a run-down battery. Indeed, something like this may well happen neurologically: the resources needed to keep the mind focused on a particular problem are apparently deficient and soon exhausted. This phenomenon is often observed in Down's-syndrome children, and is probably connected with maldevelopment of the central nervous system. The affected child does not *say* he is tired, probably because he does not feel fatigue or distaste for the subject matter.

Unfortunately, the tendency has been to give up on these children and to accept their retardation. The fact is, however, that during the short while that such a child can concentrate he learns well. The remedial program should therefore consist of a succession of very short spells of work, to be terminated at the first signs of fading out. The intervening periods of recuperation might consist of light conversation, arranging the materials for the next few moments of effort, or doing a simple puzzle. In some games, such as most of those in *Learning about Number,* the periods of effort are naturally diluted in this way.

There has been very little research into this mental fading out and how to handle it. It should be the subject of meticulous study with a stop-watch in order to find out the optimum schedule of effort and recuperation, and which types of low-stress, gamelike activities may prevent or delay its onset. It may be found that, as with petit mal seizures—in which the fading of concentration may be an allied or virtually identical phenomenon—the time needed to reestablish organized mental functioning is very small, and that the fading out does not occur during highly motivated activities of a playlike character, even though they demand uninterrupted concentration. (The 8-year-old girl playing the *Touch Card* game—with good concentration—in the film "Johnny Can Learn to Read" had petit mal seizures every two or three minutes, but only when she was relaxed or up against a difficulty. She rode around on her bicycle for an hour each day without ever falling off.)

(O)   HE/SHE DOESN'T SEEM AWARE OF WHAT THE TASK CALLS FOR

This should be treated strictly as a teacher's report. Accurate though it may be, it does not justify an assumption of "low intelligence" or "mental deficiency." These terms are not only conceptually vague, but to revert to them as an explanation of a child's failure of mental functioning means that we inquire no further and hence find out nothing about its causes.

The first step in our inquiry is to note what other descriptions the teacher has marked for the child. The above fault is seldom the only one. The apparent non-awareness may be the retreat of an unforthcoming or very dependent child into retardation or a defense against the handicap of a severe speech defect. It may also arise from the bewilderment of a child thrown into a foreign culture that makes more demands upon him than he can cope with. Such reactions produce a genuine inhibition of mental function that results in non-awareness.

Even when the non-awareness has a neurological cause it does not help to make a diagnosis of mental deficiency and leave it at that. The state of mental disorganization or sluggishness may be caused by a poisoning or malnutrition of the central nervous system, as seen in phenylketonuria and untreated thyroid deficiency. The same occurs to a less degree with drug sedation, and probably in the numerous cases of dullness associated with infected tonsils, adenoids, and ears. Therefore, the indication is for a very thorough medical examination by a *specialist*.

In the remedial situation the important thing is to find something that the child *can* do and to proceed from there. The breakthrough with Jean—the apparently severely retarded child referred to above (Stott, 1976), who used her retardation as a form of exercising dependency—came when she pushed together the two halves of one of the Two-Piece Puzzles. Our experience has been that if the child can succeed with this first item of the Flying Start the chances are that he or she can progress through the whole learning-to-learn program. The secret of treatment is never to accept apparent unawareness as representing the limit of the child's capabilities.

(P) HE/SHE PREFERS HIS OWN WAY OF DOING THINGS, WHICH OFTEN DOESN'T WORK OUT

Children in this section are also often diagnosed as "hyperactive," and indeed their behavior in the classroom can be objectively disruptive. They are in effect creative, gifted children who as adults may make valuable contributions to our civilization if they can be set on the right road to learning. What they value most is their independence—doing their own thing. Not doing the teacher's thing becomes a matter of principle. Some of them learn to read and to study on their own, others ignore the basic skills and develop artistic talents or a wide general knowledge. If they are allowed to pursue an idiosyncratic course they will become social as well as educational problems and be unable to develop their talents. Consequently, a permissive, unstructured curriculum is not suitable for them.

We regularly had a few such children in every kindergarten group of high-risk children referred to the Center. The key to their treatment is that they have an exceedingly highly developed need for personal effectiveness and uniqueness. Therefore one has to flatter their ability, pointing out that they could learn to read in a very short time and elaborating on how much more they would be able to find out once they can do so. They should then be put into a systematic and intensive reading program. They will probably also need some guidance in their relations with other children because of their wanting to dominate.

Once they have mastered the basic skills, they should be exposed to a challenging curriculum. One of the weaknesses of a public elementary system of education is the temptation to hold back creative, gifted children to the general level. If they cannot achieve the progressive effectiveness that their temperament demands within the framework of the school curriculum these children will be bored and insulted, and they will seek fulfillment elsewhere in possibly undesirable ways. One hears many accounts of their becoming behavior problems. It may not be advisable to place children of this sort in a grade much above their years because they are likely to arouse resentment and to suffer at the hands of older pupils. The solution is to organize classes at all year-levels into informal groups according to the requirements of each learning activity (not formal groups, which can become grades within grades or streams within streams). A group might well consist of children of greatly varying ability, each playing different roles within the common learning activities. This gives scope for the intellectually ambitious child to stretch himself, and for the dominant child to take a positive lead.

A class that is advancing at a uniform level is one that under-utilizes the learning potentiality of the gifted, creative child. In a Grade One class one ought to find some children who are much ahead of the others and are being encouraged to move further ahead. A few may already be good readers, others may be develop-ing thoughtfulness in mathematics. It is a pretty good guess that if such children are not found in a Grade One class—unless it serves an exclusively underprivileged neighborhood—the teacher is not encouraging such racing ahead and is probably restricting it. This writer was recently told about a child in Grade One who had been three years in a Montessori school and already read up to the Grade Two standard. She was kept busy filling page after page of a workbook by copying letters of the alphabet. Her solution to the drudgery was to make each letter so perfect that she in fact got behind in completing the pages! The excessive use of these workbooks—common in Canadian schools—to which children as well as teachers become addicted because they afford spurious completion goals, should be the telltale signal of a marching-in-step philosophy of teaching.

CHAPTER ELEVEN

The Transferability of the Learning-to-Learn Training

If statistical applications in the field of psychology
are to have any value whatsoever,
they must be preceded by
and also supplemented by observation and interpretation,
and the more exact these can be made
the better.
Sir Frederic Bartlett

This chapter reports three experiments to test the extent to which gains in learning skills made in the Flying Start program are transferred, first, to learning and problem-solving activities of a different character, and, second, to the child's learning skills in the regular classroom.

A TORONTO STUDY / by Marie J. O'Neill

This study was designed to evaluate a method of developing better learning strategies in young children considered at risk for learning disabilities, broadly defined as ineffective approaches to learning situations. The Flying Start, a programmed kit designed to help children learn to learn (Stott, 1970), was at the time in an experimental stage of development. A controlled, evaluative study was required as evidence of the validity of the method.

The Design of the Study

The population from which the sample was taken consisted of some 450 children attending Junior and Senior Kindergartens in two schools of the Borough of North York (Toronto). The neighborhood in which the schools were situated was classified as inner-city, and consisted mostly of high-density apartment blocks housing an unstable population, including many one-parent and transient families and recent immigrants. The experiment was conducted during the winter, which fortunately restricted mobility and ensured reliable school attendance.

In January of the year of the study the teachers of the ten kindergarten classes had the *Guide to the Child's Learning Skills* explained to them and were given directions about how to complete it. In the course of the next month, I, as the experimenter, made several visits to each classroom while the teachers were considering which children to refer on the basis of the Guide. They nominated 79, of whom 71 were attending school and available for testing. The criterion for acceptance into the sample was that a child should have at least one of the sections of the Guide indicating faults of learning style marked as "severe," or at least two marked as "definite." All but four of the nominated children met this criterion. The remaining 67 children were randomly allocated to Flying Start, Traditional Kindergarten, and Control groups at each of the Junior and Senior Kindergarten levels. Their age range was from 4.2 to 6.1 years. Two children in the Traditional Junior group subsequently had to be dropped because of non-availability, making a final sample of 65.

Three tests were administered, at an interval of eight weeks, before and after the teaching period. These are described below.

The experimental children were divided into eight groups of from four to six members and were taught for twelve twice-weekly sessions of half an hour over six weeks. Four groups, consisting of two at the Senior and two at the Junior Kindergarten level, were trained on the Flying Start program (described in Appendix B of this book), and similar groups were given a highly structured traditional kindergarten program as used in the Toronto Board of Education, described in full in the original monograph (O'Neill, 1975). The aims of this program include the development of sensory discrimination and training in problem-solving and good work habits. Consequently, the program shared some of the objectives of the Flying Start with regard to the fostering of learning skills. The question at issue in the experiment was whether or not the Flying Start would achieve this objective better than a well-conceived but traditional kindergarten program. Because I taught both groups myself, no teacher variable was involved.

The only exposure of the Control groups to the experimental procedures was in the pre- and post-testing. In effect, the testing itself provided an experimental hazard because of its incidental training effect. It will be seen that the Junior Control group reduced their scores on the GCLS by more than a half and the Senior by 28%, so that evidently the attention, thought, and confidence in problem-solving required by the testing were in a measure transferred to their classroom learning.

The Testing Procedures

The validation of the learning-to-learn effect of the Flying Start was complicated by the lack of test instruments designed to test learning skills. That which seemed most nearly to meet the need was the misleadingly named "Conformity Score" abstracted by Porteus, Barclay, Culver, and Kleman (1960) from part of the Porteus Maze Test. They regarded it as a test of deviant personality, having observed that delinquents tended to produce abnormal tracks on the Mazes. Broadly speaking, "good" scores were awarded when the subject followed a flexible, economical track at a particular angle of a maze. "Poor" scores were earned either if the track was unsystematic, that is, not following the path consistently, or if it followed the angle too rigidly. The minimal behavioral interpretation of these deviations would be that an unsystematic track results from the subject's not exercising sufficient attention or foresight; a rigid subservience to the angle without taking advantage of the breadth of the path to cut the corner would suggest lack of confidence in problem-solving. In short, both extremes would reflect poor learning and problem-solving skills. Indeed the "Conformity Score" would be better named "A Test of Coping Style."

The method of scoring devised by Porteus and his co-workers consisted in the matching of the angles against criterion models. Because of the possibility of scorer bias in such a procedure, I employed two independent scorers, who achieved an inter-scorer reliability correlation of 0.7231. This was acceptable but not high; however, because they worked "blind" their divergences would have worked against the significance of the results, which is methodologically permissible.

Two other tests were administered, the results of which are not reported because they are not unambiguous measures of learning style. However they have to be mentioned because they no doubt contributed to the general effect of the testing mentioned above by providing a fortuitious training in problem-solving skills.

The first was the Marble Sorter Test of Effectiveness-Motivation used by Stott and Albin (1975). It requires the child to shake marbles through floors of holes graded so that, with sufficient persistence, the marbles become sorted by color. The task requires attention to the progress of the sorting, so that some problem-solving skill is involved, but chiefly it measures the child's determination to achieve a perfort sorting, and finally to secure the seating of the marbles on the holes through which they are too large to pass. It had proved a useful test of effectiveness-motivation, but for this reason must have contained an element of constancy that limited its value as a measure of change.

The third measure was the "choices" score of Raven's Progressive Matrices. It consists of the number of overt responses the child makes before making his final decision. However, in view of the way the test was administered following Raven's instructions, it is doubtful if an increase in the number of preliminary trials can be interpreted as an improvement in learning style. It could show increased reflectivity; on the other hand, it could reflect hesitancy, or attempts to pick up cues from the tester. Moreover, the tester is required to challenge each response the child makes, which may have undermined the confidence of some by intimating that they were in error.

The chief means of assessing the transferability of the learning-to-learn effect of the Flying Start was by the diminution of faulty learning behaviors as recorded by the teachers on the GCLS. Two inter-group comparisons were made. The first was the ratio of pre/post incidence, that is to say, by how much the child's initial score, obtained before the training began, exceeded the final score obtained after the testing had finished. The second consisted in the proportion of children in each group who ended by being completely clear of faults of learning style.

Apart from the quantitative assessments of improvement in learning style, the monograph in which the study was formally reported (O'Neill, 1975) contains 20 case studies describing the progress made by a selection of the children from the Flying Start and Traditional groups. They were the counterpart of what Bricker (1970) called "frame-by-frame analysis of the performance." Some children showed remarkable changes in behavior, obvious to both the evaluator and the classroom teacher, after the third half-hour session. Teachers noted such changes at this stage for six Flying Start subjects, although one regressed. Among the

Traditional case studies, only one subject demonstrated this rapid change. Other children seemed to be immediately ready at the first session to apply themselves and to reap the maximum benefits from the programs. Stott would attribute such effects to different reasons for the poor learning behavior, the expectation being that children who were able to achieve a rapid adjustment were suffering a less severe handicap than those whose recovery was slower.

Four of the case histories are reproduced below (the case numbers relate to those given in the next section). The first is that of Joan (No. 19), an unforthcoming child who developed the excellent learning strategies that are typical of such children once they gain confidence in their abilities. The second, Claude (No. 13), was one of those who took to the program immediately and transferred his new attitudes to the classroom. Ryan (No. 18) was an extreme and confirmed hyperactive child who anomalously had excellent problem-solving skills in his quiet intervals. Angus (No. 14) moved from a pattern of aimless and disorganized behavior that suggested mild retardation to one of systematic, well-motivated work.

Effect of Known Handicaps
upon Response to the Flying Start Program

It was not possible, for lack of case histories, to examine the reasons why the children in question had poor learning skills, but a number of handicaps became apparent in the course of my contact with them. Account was taken only of those of a definitive nature. They consisted of the following:

Behavior disturbance—maladaptation to the classroom situation resulting in the child's creating bad consequences for himself or failing to use opportunities.
Health handicap—known defects of a handicapping nature.
Neurological disorder—known disorders, including lack of voluntary bladder control and incoordination.
Social deprivation—extreme neglect or known abuse.

The effect of the above was judged by the extent of improvement in learning style in response to the Flying Start program. This rating was made independently by me as the teacher of the children during the sessions and by their regular teachers, on a six-point scale (0 = no improvement, 5 = completely successful remediation). Agreement between the two sets of ratings was close: sixteen of the twenty-three were identical and five differed by one point. The only two children for whom the ratings were seriously discrepant came from the same classroom, where the main activity was free play and the teacher's philosophy was that it was difficult to assess children in the learning situation at the junior kindergarten level because her children were not learning, but playing. This attitude must have made it difficult for her to give effective ratings for improvement of learning style.

Table 1 analyzes the speed and extent of the improvement of the five children classified as hyperactive, and that of five "isolates." It is seen that the rate of progress of the former was either slow but significant or poor, but two of them were significantly improved by the end of the experiment. The one who made the least progress showed signs of neurological impairment. None made no progress. The five isolates did much better, only two making little progress as shown on the Guide (despite a 5 given one child by the teacher as her impression of improvement). The improvement of two was rated as complete, meaning that the Guide showed them by the end of the training period to be completely clear of faulty learning behaviors.

Obviously, a more extensive study with finer assessments of behavior disturbance is needed before the extent of such handicaps can be confidently assessed. It must also be borne in mind that the total treatment consisted of only twelve half-hour sessions over six weeks. If a hyperactive child makes only a little improvement over so short a period this must be reckoned as encouraging.

Table 2 shows the response of the nine children who were socially deprived to the extent of extreme neglect or known abuse. Considering that all but one had other handicaps, as a group they did surprisingly well. Three improved rapidly and four slowly but significantly. Three, including two of the latter, were completely clear of faulty learning behaviors as rated on the Guide at the end of the training period, and three showed significant improvement. Judgment has to be withheld about the deterioration of case No. 5 in view of what was said above about the teacher's attitude to kindergarten education. The rate of improvement for this deprived group was only slightly less than that of the not severely deprived group.

The General Learning-to-Learn Effect as Measured by the GCLS

The pre/post ratios of improvement in learning style for each of the three groups are given in Table 3. Among the Senior Kinder-

Table 1. Improvement of behavior-disturbed children

Group	Case no.	Other known handicap	Rating of improvement in learning style by		Assessment of speed of improvement by experimenter	Extent of final improvement as assessed by teacher on guide
			Experimenter	Teacher		
Hyperactive						
	7	—	4	4	slow but significant	significant
	18	neurological signs	2	1	poor	little
	20	—	3	3	slow but significant	little
	21	health & deprivation	5	4	slow but significant	significant
	22	health & deprivation	3	3	poor	little
Isolate						
	2	health	5	5	rapid	complete
	6	elective mute & deprivation	4	4	rapid	significant
	8	—	3	2	poor	little
	14	deprivation	5	5	poor	little
	19	deprivation	5	4	slow but significant	complete

Table 2. Improvement of deprived children (extreme neglect or known abuse)

Case no.	Other known handicap	Rating of improvement in learning style by		Assessment of speed of improvement by experimenter	Extent of final improvement as assessed by teacher on guide
		Experimenter	Teacher		
3	health	4	3	rapid	significant
5	health & neurological signs	5	0[a]	slow but significant	worse[a]
9	—	4	4	slow but significant	complete
6	behavioral (elective mute)	4	4	rapid	significant
14	behavioral (isolate)	5	5	rapid	complete
18	behavioral (hyperactive) neurological signs	2	1	poor	little
19	behavioral (isolate)	5	4	slow but significant	complete
21	health	5	4	slow but significant	significant
22	health	3	3	poor	little

[a]See text for explanation of discrepancies.

Table 3. Relative incidence of faulty learning behaviors shown as ratios pre- and post-training

	Junior	Senior
Flying Start	2.26	3.63
Traditional	4.05	2.16
Control	2.09	1.38

garten children (ages 5–6 years), the greatest improvement, measured by remission of faulty learning behaviors, was shown by the Flying Start group. Among the Juniors (ages 4–5 years) it was greatest among those following the Traditional Kindergarten program. This is of interest, since the Flying Start was originally developed and field-tested with 5–6-year-old children.

When the number of children showing a complete remission of faulty learning behaviors is taken as a criterion, the results for the Flying Start group were consistently better than those for the other two groups. These results are shown in Table 4. It is seen that five of the eleven Senior Flying Start subjects showed a complete remission of faulty learning behaviors, compared with two of the eleven Traditional and one of the twelve Control subjects.

Transfer of the Learning-to-Learn Effect as Shown by the Porteus Conformity Score

The mean gains, as measured by the Porteus Conformity score described above, were 3.7 for the Flying Start, 0.67 for the Traditional, and 0.0 for the Control groups, the superiority of the

Table 4. Numbers and percentages of children free of faulty learning behaviors by the end of the training period

	Junior		Senior		Totals	
	No.	%	No.	%	No.	%
Flying Start	5/12	42	5/11	45	10/23	43
Traditional	3/9	33	2/11	18	5/20	25
Control	3/10	30	1/12	8	4/22	18

Flying Start over each of the other groups being significant at the 0.05 level. Again the Senior Flying Start group showed the greatest improvement; their scores moved from the areas of disorganization and rigidity to moderate flexibility, reflecting a more reasoned and reflective approach.

Comments on the Evaluation

The Flying Start is both a method and a program. The programmed materials allow children at risk to bring into play little-used abilities that permit the development of good learning strategies. Moreover, the program has sufficient flexibility to accommodate a reasonably wide range of individual differences. Under favorable conditions, these modes of attack in problem-solving generalize to the classroom situation. As a result, classroom behavior is seen to be more purposeful, orderly, and mature, and consequently more acceptable.

In this study the experimenter was both conducting a formative evaluation of the Flying Start program and attempting to encourage significant changes in the subjects. Problems discovered in administering the Flying Start with any particular set of children had to be remedied on the spot, or the new way of dealing with the materials would be put into action at the next session with different children, following Guralnick's (1973) research-service model for the evaluation of learning materials. The variability of response between children of four and five years of age further complicated the process. The changes made in the course of the evaluation appear to have favored the Senior groups.

Another feature of variability of response affecting the evaluative process is the composition of the small groups. These groups contained mixtures of under- and over-reactive children, bringing with them inappropriate response sets to the learning situation. In addition, the children came from different classrooms and usually did not know each other. Adaptation to the experimental situation was extremely difficult for a few of these children. In fact, some children were not sufficiently flexible to adjust to work with the other children in their groups. However, they were able to improve their learning strategies with the support of the experimenter on a one-to-one basis, thus making a beginning in the establishment of a cooperative approach to the learning situation.

The occurrence of children in the Flying Start groups whose development of adequate responses to treatment was slow may be related to features of the experimental design. Two half-hour sessions per week for only six weeks under the above conditions is evidently insufficient for slow responders. For these children there was no obvious follow-on of the activity in the classroom, since—in order to retain the "blind" aspect of the experimental design—the teachers were not informed of the nature of the interventions used. One teacher became acutely aware of the improvement in learning style of two or three of the Flying Start group, and noticeably changed her classroom methods. Post-experimentally this teacher recorded very few items of faulty behavior for any of her children, including the Controls.

From the evaluator's point of view, the Flying Start was more satisfactory to administer than the Traditional program. Positive changes in learning behaviors of children were observable during the course of the Flying Start program, whereas several of the older Traditional subjects appeared at times to exhibit the same non-productive behavior in the sessions that was seen by the teacher in the classroom. These were over-reactive children who would seek alternative activities when they had finished their set task. When alternatives for action were not available, these children would often regress to fidgety and sometimes disruptive behavior. Children in Flying Start groups, on the other hand, had recourse to a variety of materials and could be further deployed as helpers with slower members, thus increasing their cooperativeness and further developing their attentional and problem-solving skills.

The Case Histories

The solid histograms at the top of each case history indicate the severity of each poor learning style (0–3) as recorded by the teacher before the training period. The broken histograms (used actually only for the fourth case) show the same after the end of the training. The capital letters refer to the categories of poor learning styles in the *Guide to the Child's Learning Skills*.

Joan (Age: 5.4)

Although not mute, Joan was extremely shy. She froze when approached (A) and would barely answer her teacher in a whisper. She had no friends, perhaps because she did not speak to any of the children. When given work to do, she was sometimes able to rise to the occasion, but in open situations she tended to be easily distracted (D). Without guidance, Joan would sit, apparently unable or unwilling to initiate any activity (K). Sometimes she would hide in a corner of the room and be found sitting there in a miserable state.

It was obvious to the teacher from the infrequent work Joan produced that the child was potentially quite competent, but that her withdrawn behavior was arresting her development as an efficient learner.

Joan did not speak to the experimenter during the pre-experimental visits, although she smiled shyly from a distance and established eye contact. The tester found the child so apprehensive that at first it was difficult for her to function in the testing situation. However, she rallied and made an effort to cooperate on all tests, without uttering a word.

The Senior Kindergarten Flying Start group to which Joan belonged included two other children from her home room, which made her departure for the experimental room quite smooth. Joan chose to sit next to the only other girl in the group, although she did not look at her or speak to her. On the first day, she finished all the work given to her quickly, accurately, and without comment. Having completed a puzzle, she would sit looking straight ahead until her work was changed. When praised for her efforts, she would drop her head on her chest. During the second session, Joan worked with the other girl in the group to form Merry-go-Rounds and to play Mail Boxes. The play was quite intense and precise. Joan once more said nothing during the session, and was not pressed to respond verbally. She did not resort to dropping her head when addressed at this second session, but instead looked at the experimenter and began to smile faintly.

From that session onward Joan moved through the work with great efficiency. She seldom made mistakes with her work, or she corrected them herself if she did. Verbal responses from her in the small group were generally monosyllabic, so the experimenter encouraged other children to fill in for her where stories on the What's Happening games were required. Joan paid good attention to these stories, and appeared to enjoy the communion with other members of the group.

By the end of the series, the teacher was reporting that Joan had dropped her withdrawn behavior, and was now willing to talk to her without embarrassment. She no longer hid away, but could join in group activities, having acquired one or two friends.

Discussion.   This child was able to take advantage of the highly structured sequential learning situation. Through it she was able to reveal a reflective, highly competent mode of adaptive behavior, which her teacher suspected was available. At her own speed, and without pressure, Joan emerged from her withdrawn shell to proceed as a fairly normal child quite able to cope with the large open classroom situation because she had now mastered ways of using her potential. Under these circumstances, with adequate support in her home room, Joan's unprofitable non-adaptive behaviors dropped away.

Claude (Age: 6.0)

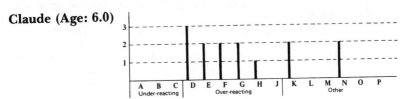

Claude could not adapt to the situation that existed in his classroom. The teacher saw him as over-active (D), impulsive (E), fidgety (F), and somewhat unpredictable (G). He also lost interest in the work that she set (N), and appeared quite uninterested (K) in the ongoing program.

He was not shy when visited in his classroom, but, equally, he was not very interested in visitors. The tester received a similar response. However, Claude was willing to go along with the tester, and cooperated very well on all tests, demonstrating an intelligent approach to all items.

Claude took to the experimental program surprisingly well. Always somewhat serious, he approached every stage with a zeal that belied his profile. He demonstrated the utmost care and patience, and was able to cooperate well with other members of the group, although he showed a preference for one of his classmates, whose profile was similar, but who progressed at a rapid rate in the Flying Start program.

There was no dramatic point of recovery for Claude, because from the outset he adapted so well. It was noticed, however, that in the second week of the experiment, i.e., after three lessons, Claude's teacher began to refer to him as a model member of her class. Apparently he had settled down to the conditions of the classroom and was using his new skills to make work for himself that the teacher saw to be productive.

Discussion. It became clear during the experimental program that Claude was capable of performing in a highly effective manner, although he had appeared to the teacher to be quite disorganized. It is likely that he had been reacting against the open setting of his classroom, in which he had initially been unable to function to his own satisfaction.

Angus (Age: 5.11)

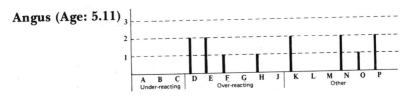

On visits to the classroom one sometimes notices the peripheral child. He is pleasant and does not cause any fuss, but he does not join in any activities unless pressed, and then he does so as if in a daze. Angus was such a child. He would wander around the room touching things but seeming to take little notice either of the things touched or of anything that was going on.

His teacher reported that Angus would not reflect, but would rather guess (D) if he bothered to answer at all (K), that he seemed out of contact with the classroom situation (N, O), that he would leave work unfinished, or that he would insist on performing in his own invariant manner (P) as if he paid no heed to the teacher's instructions.

However, Angus did seem to take notice of the novel human stimulus. Whenever the experimenter entered the room, Angus would edge towards her side of the room and stand limply watching her, with his head at an odd angle, somewhat like a curious puppy, and he would have a strange half-smile on his face. When spoken to, Angus only broadened his smile and would not answer.

The tester found Angus quite willing to go along to the test room, although he proved very shy, and did not speak at all during testing. He also scored below his age level on both the Porteus and Raven tests, and he made only a mediocre attempt at sorting.

Angus was not too shy to join the group on the way to the small room, although he kept his distance, walking with his shoulders slumped and his head at this odd uncomfortable angle. With his flaccid appearance and inactive approach to the school situation, and without reference to pre-test results, one would easily be led into judging him a candidate for the school for the retarded. In fact, a note "Query Rubinstein Syndrome" was made at the first observation session, because of his strangeness and triangle-shaped face.

Angus eventually corrected this misconception. In the first lesson he showed an ability to listen, to understand, and to follow directions. He was still, in this first lesson, operating as a non-motivated, apparently slow, and somewhat sloppy worker who required instruction at each step of the way. Before the second lesson Angus was found in the classroom in his habitual stance, idling around the room, head to one side. During the second lesson, he was given a Merry-go-Round puzzle and instructed in its use with another child. He followed the method precisely, and suddenly began to be very particular about the placement of pieces. He began to complete sections of the work so swiftly that he was already able to select his own materials.

On the third day Angus came hurrying over to the experimenter when she appeared at the door. There was not much change in him to notice on the way to the experiment room; he still showed the same slow movement along the passages, with his head to one side. However, his approach to the work that day became masterful. He was finishing work as quickly as it could be laid out, even though he was working with ultimate carefulness, following the rules of the game precisely. That day Angus finished all the materials available, and was then quite happy to select materials and to show other children how to work with them. Angus returned to his room transformed. Nothing was said to the teacher, but the change in the boy was so startling that the teacher asked what had "been done" to him.

The improvement continued both in the experimental sessions and in the classroom. Angus did not become very talkative, but he began to ask for work, and to offer to discuss the materials he was using. The veneer of semi-retardation dropped away and Angus became a cooperative, avid worker, persistent in his efforts to complete work with the utmost care. He remained somewhat solitary, but this was accepted in the classroom, since it was clear that he was using his time in healthy pursuits. As his profile shows, the teacher found no reason to question his performance or ability by the end of the experiment.

Discussion. Angus benefited very greatly from the experimental program. Because of an intense interest in the materials, his amount of practice during the sessions exceeded that of the average group member, and this no doubt influenced the total effect, which was clearly remarkable by the third session. Perhaps the intensity of Angus' response is needed for full advantage to be taken of such a program. When this does occur, there is no doubt that the effects generalize, even without the knowledge on the part of those who by rights are needed to give back-up support to the efforts of the child. Angus was fortunate in having a teacher who observed the change in his learning strategies and encouraged him. She did this by permitting him to develop his individual style in his home room program, and to explore his environment in a manner that was obviously motivating him to further achievement.

Ryan (Age: 5.4)

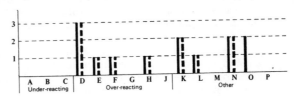

Ryan was like a miniature car on permanent overdrive. Short but husky, he was never still. He would race around the classroom during much of the school day, following the teacher, always demanding attention, never stopping to think before acting (D). He would often haul himself up onto the table tops and run around from table to table, laughing, just out of reach of the teacher. He would only work for seconds at a time even when closely supervised. He quickly became distracted (E, N), was fidgety (F), and seemed to have little idea of his responsibilities in the teacher-pupil relationship (O).

He was too involved in his compulsive running around to take much notice of the experimenter on her visits. At first he would run past, yelling "Hi!" On later visits he would stop for a second to ask why the stranger was there. Then he would be off to another part of the room.

Ryan treated the testing session very lightly. He was impatient with listening to instructions, especially for the Raven Test. He rushed ahead on the task and then gave up abruptly before finishing the second set. He enjoyed the sorting task, particularly the noise.

Ryan hopped and jumped and skipped his way to the first of the experimental sessions. He belonged to a Flying Start group. He was interested in the materials from the beginning, showing skill in putting together, without error, any of the puzzles presented to him. He needed no help. He would make a puzzle, then rush around the room looking at everyone else's work. He worked so quickly that it was impossible to check his work before he was away again. He was told that he could select his own work, but he would not do this. Instead, he would ask for a drink of water or to go to the bathroom, or he would head for the door or run around on the table-tops.

It was possible to bring these behaviors under partial control. Ryan responded to being asked to help the experimenter or another child, and he learned to remain in the room during the sessions. He did not, however, settle down long enough during any one period to become absorbed in the work, nor did he ever learn to switch activities on his own initiative. Nevertheless, in fragments of time, Ryan successfully worked his way through all of the materials, sometimes showing genuine enjoyment.

Discussion.   At the conclusion of the experiment some enquiries were made concerning Ryan's health. His hyperactivity was so marked that both the teacher and the experimenter felt that medical opinion should be sought. Unfortunately the parents did not respond to the inquiry, so that no conclusions may be drawn in this regard. Ryan appeared to be perfectly coordinated, and he had demonstrated that he was potentially capable of academic development. The reasons for his extraordinary drive remain a matter for conjecture.

There is some evidence to show that the Flying Start program assisted Ryan in the development of his learning strategies, because after the series of lessons he was no longer able to pass off the impression that he did not understand the learning situations in his classroom. However, because Ryan was still spending much of his time in disruptive, non-constructive hyperactivity, it must be stated that for Ryan the program had no real force.

[The reader is also referred to the discussion of Ryan in the latter part of Chapter Four, where it is suggested that his is a case of excessive effectiveness-motivation. The Flying Start was only of value to him diagnostically, in making it clear that he was not a typical hyperactive. He needed something much more challenging and difficult, such as an intensive course in reading or mathematics. As a child completes the Flying Start he should progress to the reading and math games, but the across-group design of Dr O'Neill's experiment precluded this.—D.H.S.]

A SCOTTISH STUDY / by George O. B. Thomson

The objectives of this study were: 1) to evaluate the *Guide to the Child's Learning Skills* (GCLS) as a teacher-based instrument for screening and follow-up, and 2) to determine the efficacy of the Flying Start materials in modifying inappropriate learning behavior.

In recent years the Stott hypothesis has gained in credibility and currency. Simply enunciated, the hypothesis is that learning failure may be a product of inappropriate behaviors in the learning situation rather than of low level of cognitive performance, and that what we should do as educational psychologists, remedial teachers, etc., is look not at test scores but at the child's problem-solving behavior and subsequently monitor progress and note crucial points of improvement. The *Guide to the Child's Learning Skills* was designed for the classroom identification of children who use faulty approaches to learning, which may be caused by temperamental, cultural, or neurological factors or a combination of handicapping events.

Throughout the Spring and Autumn terms of 1974/75, a series of pilot studies was carried out in schools in the Edinburgh area in order to ascertain teachers' reactions to the Guide and its suitability for assessing children's problem-solving approaches, and to try out various ways of organizing groups to use the Flying Start materials in Infant classrooms. It was found that the Guide did serve a very useful purpose in helping teachers to be more precise in their description of learning behaviors, notably those that are inimical to the learning process. Most of the criticisms made of the Guide by teachers in the pilot studies have since been met in the version of the Guide currently used. It was further ascertained that the Guide offered a basis for identifying children at risk for learning problems. The criterion of "at risk" was held to be: those children who scored one or more "severe" signs or two or more "definite" signs on the Guide.

Central to this study is the hypothesis that children so identified by the GCLS and exposed to a program of structured games like the Flying Start should demonstrate significantly altered problem-solving approaches when compared with other groups. Furthermore, any such change should be reflected in significantly improved learning behavior profiles recorded by teachers. This raises the question of assessing the aptness of the problem-solving behaviors used. Standardized test scores cannot apply the information required for a detailed and ongoing analysis of change in this critical variable. What was needed was a measure of changes in the *modes of attack* in the problem-solving situation.

As a result of the pilot studies, two non-verbal tests were selected in view of the possibility that some of the subjects would refuse to respond verbally in testing situations and that the actions of pointing, drawing, etc., would be less threatening. The tests chosen were the Porteus Maze Test V and the Columbia Mental Maturity Scale (CMMS).

The Porteus Maze Test yielded two scores: the usual test quotient and a score measuring flexibility or adaptation, already described by Dr. O'Neill in the first part of this chapter.

The CMMS not only assesses the level of mental functioning but also offers an opportunity to observe the use of strategies of rehearsal/reflectivity.

Children who have been exposed to the Flying Start program will have been trained to become strategy-wise in the learning situations. Central to the behavioral approach to learning failure is the view that children's faulty learning behaviors are largely the reflection of inadequacies in their manner of coping with day-to-day situations. If more efficient learning styles have been developed by means of the Flying Start program, the improvements should be transferred to classroom learning. This result should then be apparent in four ways:

1. The children receive fewer and less serious markings by their teachers on the GCLS.
2. Because children working with the Flying Start materials will receive specific training in planning and problem-solving strategies, their ability to plan ahead should be demonstrated by improved scores on tasks that require such skills. In particular, their Porteus Maze Test quotient scores should show an increase.
3. Additionally, children trained in planning strategies should approach a problem requiring planning in a relaxed manner, which should result in work that is relatively well adapted to its objective rather than disorganized, irregular, or over-conforming. Therefore, such children should show greater

changes in the Porteus score measuring flexibility and adaptability.

4. Children receiving specific training in the value of deliberating over decision-making should show an increased score on Columbia Mental Maturity Scale.

The Design of the Experiment

The sample was drawn from the 145 children attending first-year primary classes in four schools in the Borders region of Scotland in August, 1975.

A period was allowed for the children to get used to the experimenter, and the teachers to get to know the children and to familiarize themselves with the GCLS. They completed this phase toward the end of November, and by the above criteria, 34 at risk children were identified.

There was no marked variation in the teachers' individual preferences for one category of fault, but, as Beilin (1959) noted, they collectively identified a greater amount of over-reacting than of under-reacting behaviors.

The high-risk children were divided randomly into Experimental (E) and Control (C) groups. Their mean scores for each category of faulty learning style were very similar. All were pretested on the Porteus Maze V and the CMMS. I then worked with them, in eight groups (four E and four C) in their schools for two half-hour sessions over eight weeks, sixteen sessions in all. With the E groups I used the Flying Start materials as recommended in the manual, supervising their play in pairs. With the C groups I used play materials not available to the E groups or to the rest of the class, comprising jigsaw puzzles, letter bingo, concept cards, etc. Both C and E groups thus received the same individual attention but were exposed to different experiences.

At the end of the eight-week period, the Guide was completed by the teachers for each of the 34 children and the CMMS and Porteus Maze V were readministered.

Results

Table 5 shows the mean pre- and post-training scores on the three tests for which results are available to date. (Those for the Porteus Conformity will be the subject of a subsequent report using an objec-

Table 5. Mean pre- and post-training scores on the tests used

Group	Pre	Post	Change	t	p
California Mental Maturity Scale					
Flying Start (E)	87.0	100.8	+13.8	4.83	<.01
Controls (C)	87.7	90.3	+ 2.6	0.80	ns
Porteus Maze Quotients					
Flying Start (E)	88.69	97.06	+ 8.37	3.78	<.01
Controls (C)	84.44	88.79	+ 4.35	1.47	ns
Guide to the Child's Learning Skills					
Flying Start (E)	10.29	2.08	− 8.21	3.28	<.01
Controls (C)	9.35	7.88	− 1.47	1.43	ns

tive method of scoring.) It is seen that all of them showed significant improvements for the Flying Start (E) group. Although the Control group showed some improvements in score, in none of the tests did these reach the level of significance.

In the post-test of the CMMS the Flying Start group were notable for their greater response time, frequent eye-scanning movements, looking, checking, etc., and generally not blurting out their answers. The Control group showed little difference from pre-test, their behavior being marked by either inhibition or guessing.

The means for the GCLS are of the totals of scores for inappropriate learning styles, ranging for each category from 0 to 3. The means for the separate categories are shown in the bar-graphs of Figures 1 and 2. For the Flying Start group the falls in the categories of impulsivity (D), distractibility (E), evasion (H), and loss of concentration (N) are particularly striking.

Two Illustrative Case Histories

David was in his second year in the Infant Department. His classroom behavior was characterized by hyperactivity of a degree that disturbed even this most active of classrooms. He frequently chattered and seemed incapable of keeping his attention on one thing for any length of time. His level of achievement in the classroom was described as low, and this was certainly borne out by examination of his written and oral work. On initial assessment he scored 85 on the CMMS, and his first attempt at the Porteus Maze Test (reproduced as Figure 3) is

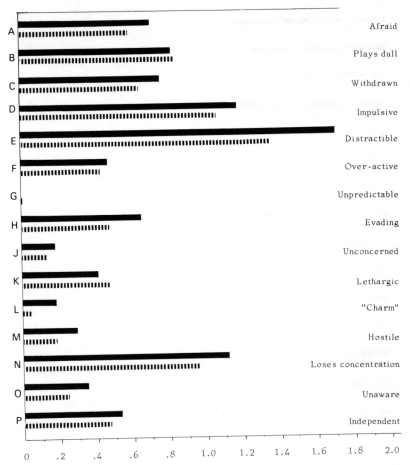

Figure 1. Mean scores for inappropriate learning styles of the control group. *Solid bars* indicate pre-training, *broken bars* indicate post-training. Maximum score per category = 3.

seen to be a highly disorganized performance, in contrast to his post-test performance (Figure 4), where a much more controlled attempt is in evidence. His pre-training learning behavior profile reflects his overreacting approach (Figure 5).

Throughout the training sessions David presented something of a management problem. Initially he would only stay still for a few minutes, but, gradually, as he became interested in the activities, he demonstrated greater control, a degree of planning, and less erratic

Figure 2. Mean scores for inappropriate learning styles of the experimental group. *Solid bars* indicate pre-training, *broken bars* indicate post-training. Maximum score per category = 3.

behavior in contrast to his behavior on first acquaintance. On post-test David's CMMS score rose to 91. His performance was characterized by greater time spent scanning the cards, inhibition of impulsive responses, and frequent eye movements, interpreted as checking and double-checking. The post-training GCLS indicated a marked decrease in over-reacting behaviors (Figure 5). As a result of these observations, the tentative conclusion offered is that David's initial inappropriate learning style had been caused more by general cultural influences than by any functional disorder.

In contrast to David's "inconsequent" behavior was Duncan's un-forthcomingness. He was excessively shy and timid. His teacher found it difficult to elicit any conversation from him and reported that he frequently burst into tears when under normal classroom pressures. He seemed to be satisfied with a static level of competence, he rarely tried, and I experienced great difficulty in establishing rapport with him in the pre-tests. His CMMS performance (with a score of 84) was characterized by frequent refusals and hesitant pointing unaccompanied by any verbal comment. The Porteus Maze Test was met by refusal (Figure 6). His general unforthcomingness is demonstrated by his pre-training learning behavior profile (Figure 8).

At the end of the sessions, Duncan showed noticeably more confidence on the CMMS, and his score increased to 100. This increased confidence is further reflected in the post-test Porteus Maze, which demonstrates a highly competent performance (Figure 7). Furthermore, the post-test behavior profile indicates a marked reduction in the degree of severity of unforthcomingness (Figure 8).

AN EAST LONDON STUDY / by Len F. Green, Sid Brown, and Jean Francis

The object of this study was to test the efficacy of alternative programs in helping children improve their learning styles. These programs were the Flying Start Learning-to-Learn Kit and the "Language" program, a series of pictures to be used as a medium for language development and perceptual discrimination. The latter included discussion by the children of their drawings.

The subjects for this study were drawn from the 91 children of three Infants classes, of ages 66–78 months, in a school serving a low socioeconomic neighborhood in East London. From these were chosen the 36 who had the largest adverse scores on the Preliminary Screening questions of the GCLS. They were divided into three groups of twelve, two groups for the two different treatments and one group to provide no-treatment controls. The allocation to the groups was done by a stranger to the children by matching for sex, age, and score. Each group consisted of six of each sex, except that one girl in the Flying Start group left the school before the experiment was completed.

The children in the Flying Start and Language groups were withdrawn in groups of four for half an hour each week for ten weeks. The Control group was given no extra help outside the classroom.

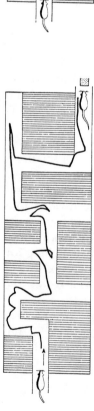

Figure 3. DAVID Porteus Maze Pre-training

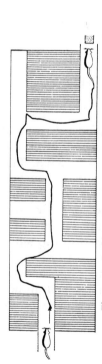

Figure 4. DAVID Porteus Maze Post-training

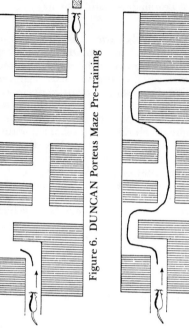

Figure 6. DUNCAN Porteus Maze Pre-training

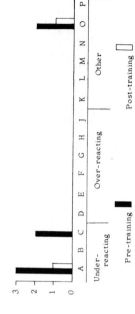

Figure 7. DUNCAN Porteus Maze Post-training

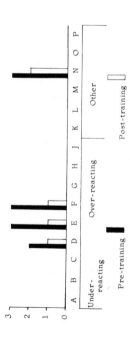

Figure 5. DAVID Inappropriate learning behavior (GCLS)

Figure 8. DUNCAN Inappropriate learning behavior (GCLS)

A fourth group, also of twelve, was made up of children who had no adverse score on the Preliminary Screening. This No-fault group was likewise given no extra help outside the classroom.

A modified version of the Raven and the Harris-Goodenough Draw-a-Man Tests were given to all four groups before the period of training and shortly after its conclusion.

The full *Guide to the Child's Learning Skills* was completed for the Flying Start group by the children's teachers before and after the period of training, but it was done for the other two groups of children with high adverse scores on the Preliminary Screening only after the training.

Results

It is seen from Table 6 that on the Raven Test the Flying Start group showed a greater pre- to post-training improvement than the other three groups in the number of correct choices. Their improvement was significant at the 0.01 level ($t = 3.99$). That of the Language group fell short of significance ($t = 1.51$), as did also that of the No-treatment group ($t = 1.33$). The small improvement of the No-fault group is explained by their having scored at near the ceiling of the Test on both occasions.

It is also seen that the Flying Start group took much less time in doing the Test as a whole, compared with the Language group, but the time taken by the No-treatment group improved by about the same amount as the Flying Start. The greater speed of the latter is

Table 6. Pre- and post-test performance on the Raven Colored Progressive Matrices

	Flying Start (11)	Language (12)	No-treatment (12)	No-fault (12)
Mean pre-test score	8.82	8.50	8.67	11.33
Mean post-test score	10.46	9.58	9.09	11.41
Mean gain	1.64	1.08	0.42	0.08
Mean difference in time taken (sec)	56.18	+0.3	−28.9	−25.7
Mean difference in time taken per correct choice (sec)	15.65	−3.5	−8.0	−2.5

better shown by the large drop in the time they took per correct choice (over 15 seconds) compared with either the Language group (3.5 seconds) or the No-treatment group (8 seconds).

On the Draw-a-Man Test (Table 7) the Language group did best, the 4.76-point improvement in their score being significant (t = 2.66) at the .05 level. The performance of the Flying Start group was actually somewhat worse on the post-test, with a drop of 3.09 points, but this did not approach significance. The No-treatment group maintained almost the same score. The improvement of the No-fault group of 3.2 was just significant at the .05 level.

The better performance of the Language group is no doubt attributable to the fact that they used pencil and paper during their language sessions, which included discussion of pictures that emphasized human physical characteristics. Therefore they received training that had a close affinity to the Draw-a-Man Test.

The pre- and post-test completion of the GCLS for the Flying Start group showed a halving of their mean adverse-mark score, from 9.36 to 4.55. This was significant at the .01 level (t = 3.169). No formal comparison can be made with the other two groups for lack of pre-test ratings. The post-test mean for the Language group was 4.42, and for the No-training group 4.17, the latter being actually slightly lower, i.e., better than that of the Flying Start group. Since the three groups were carefully matched by their adverse ratings in the Preliminary Screening, there is reason to believe that, if the Language and No-training groups had been rated on the full Guide before training, their scores would have been of the same order as those of the Flying Start group. It must therefore be reckoned that they made a comparable improvement. Although

Table 7. Pre- and post-test performance on the Harris-Goodenough Draw-a-Man Test

	Group			
	Flying Start (11)	Language (12)	No-treatment (12)	No-fault (12)
Mean pre-test score	97.1	91.4	87.4	100.3
Mean post-test score	94.0	96.2	87.6	103.4
Mean change	−3.1	+4.8	+0.2	+3.2

that of the Language group could be explained as a result of their training, it is hard to account for the improvement of the No-treatment group. It is possible that a Hawthorne effect was in operation, in that the study aroused considerable interest among the three teachers completing the Guides.

CASE DESCRIPTIONS / by Sid Brown

Maria

It was immediately apparent that, although not mute, Maria was extremely shy. When approached by a teacher (or any adult such as classroom welfare assistants, etc.) she froze (A)[1], gave every impression of being a dull child (B), and did not seem aware of what the task called for (O). Probably because of her unwillingness to speak to any one, she had no friends, although she was well-liked by her peers and many attempts were made by them to get her to join in their activities. In fact, they were perhaps over-considerate in that they would answer for her or draw her attention to something the teacher wanted but that did not appear to have registered with her. At times she did rise to the occasion on being given work to do, but in the classroom situation, more often than not, her work was just allowed to slide, and unless her teacher was vigilant she would be content to sit, apparently unwilling or unable to initiate any activity. There were times, too, when she would be found in some distant corner of the room, having gravitated there unbeknown to her teacher.

Both the headmistress of the school and other members of staff with whom Maria came into contact were firmly of the opinion that Maria had considerable potential and that the reason for her not developing as an efficient learner was her extremely withdrawn behavior.

Maria did not speak to me throughout the whole program (although I made many efforts to get her to say even "Hello!"). Her smiles became more frequent, however, and eye contact was established throughout. The first session was a difficult one because of her apprehensiveness and her not being prepared to communicate. By the following week, however, there was an improvement, and from then on she showed a willing cooperation in carrying out the Flying Start tasks, but still without speaking a single word. She had made a friend during the second session, and this was to prove to be of considerable help to both of us during the following eight sessions of the program. Indeed, from this point onwards very obvious signs of

---

[1]Letters in brackets refer to the faulty learning styles identified in the GCLS.

Maria's progress could be seen. She made fewer mistakes, and when she did make one she quickly corrected it herself or with help from her friend, who, along with other volunteers, filled in for her when verbal interaction was required, (as in telling the stories of "What's Happening?").

Maria seemed happy as a member of such a small group. She appeared to enjoy the social interaction and was able to take full advantage of the highly structured sequential learning situation. Through this she was able to reveal and confirm the existence of the potential ability her teachers had long felt she possessed. She is fortunate in having a class teacher sensitive to her new responsiveness and capable of helping her transition from the very apprehensive almost mute person she had been to someone well on the way to becoming a competent member of her class. Her teacher's notes confirm that she is emerging from her withdrawn shell and coping better every day with the large open classroom situation. Under these circumstances and with the practical support she is receiving in her own room, her faulty learning styles are very noticeably falling away.

Paul

Paul was a shy, quiet, but friendly child when he arrived for the first session. He showed a certain amount of apprehension, and this confirmed to some degree his class teacher's assessment of him as being afraid to commit himself to starting a new task (A) and also ready to assume the role of a not-so-bright child. In this session he was impulsive (D), although his class teacher's assessment makes no reference to this. He did not always conform, however, and on balance it was felt he should be classed as being disruptive of others and easily distracted himself (H). At the same time his teacher considered that his powers of concentration faded easily (N), and this was substantiated by my own observations. From the first session, his pattern of behavior, which lasted for the whole of the program, was one of cooperation, and the good relationship that developed from this allowed Paul to produce work in which it was obvious he was taking pride and which gave him a lot of satisfaction. That he was resorting less and less to impulsivity and inattention became obvious, and his changed attitude after the half-way point in the teaching program was also quite marked.

There was no doubt that Paul had responded well to the small group situation, providing as it did an opportunity for him to feel free of the pressures that can come from the more public aspects of a large open classroom. He also appreciated the order and sequence of the Flying Start activities and found satisfaction in working successfully within this framework. His class teacher's observations confirm that he has also been able to make the transition to the classroom satisfactorily and that indications of faulty learning styles D, H, and N have completely fallen away.

GENERAL COMMENTARY ON THE EXPERIMENTAL STUDIES / by D. H. Stott

As I have intimated elsewhere in this book, I have always had reservations about the formal experimental–control group type of experiment for the evaluation of teaching methods. Children are so different, and their potentialities so hidden, that the matching of the groups must always be a chancy affair. This and the varying conditions of each experiment result all too often in contradictory findings. To this must be added the risks that the findings run as they are passed on from summary to summary and book to book. Be that as it may, it is comforting to see that in the three experiments reported in this chapter the Flying Start gets a certain edge over the other forms of treatment used.

Nevertheless I consider this only a minor outcome of these studies. As Guralnick and Blackman point out, the summation of average performances hides the real effects of a treatment from the point of view of utility of the method. What the remedial teacher wishes to know is its efficacy with particular types of children. This is where the case reports are so valuable; they make it clear that the Flying Start is successful in giving confidence to unforthcoming children and in enabling them to translate their natural caution and desire for certainty into productive learning strategies, no doubt because they can succeed without the use of language. It can also wean them gently away from the strategy of feigned incompetence, as seen in Maria's reliance upon her peers to think and answer for her. In addition, the program seems to bring into use whatever powers of concentration and control the impulsive child is able to muster, and acts diagnostically in distinguishing between those whose impulsivity is caused by lack of training and those in whom it is temperamental or "organic." With the child who is hyperactive because of the inordinate demands he makes for effective interaction with his environment, the Flying Start is of value only as an opener (see my comment on Ryan at the end of Dr. Marie O'Neill's case descriptions).

Finally I should like to comment on an aspect of the studies, in particular that of Green, Brown, and Francis, that points the way to a possible new concept of intervention strategies. This is the general effect of the experiment on the population within which it is conducted. The above authors found, to their surprise, a considerable improvement in their no-treatment control group, and surmise that some kind of a Hawthorne effect might have been operating. If it is in fact true that the treatment of a minority of the children in small groups for a mere half-hour a week results in a significant improvement in the work attitudes of the whole class, surely we are on to something really important. The history of science is full of instances where an experimentalist became curious about an incidental phenomenon and made a great discovery. So let us be curious about this phenomenon. Can it be that merely having to complete a questionnaire about children's learning attitudes gives teachers more explicit goals in encouraging good learning habits in their students and noting and correcting poor habits in individuals? Even if this is only in part the answer, it suggests a new resource of teacher education.

Or, can it be that the children who are withdrawn proudly demonstrate their new-found success-achieving skills to others—or at least cease to offer social models of distractibility and despondency? It is a matter of common observation that, in any group of children, once one of them starts something, be it only a catcall or a giggle, the rest follow. Likewise, any new trick or capability is immediately copied. If the new achievement involves close attention and controlled effort, the learning strategies of the whole class will thereby be improved. My conjecture is that this is how the improvement of the no-treatment control groups is largely to be accounted for.

Experienced teachers know how important a class atmosphere is. One year a teacher will have a "good" class, the next year a "poor" class—both drawn from the same neighborhood. It would appear that a small minority of the children are able to set the tone, either of studiousness or of waywardness. No doubt there have been studies of class tone, but they are rare and I do not know of any. In some inner-city areas tone is so bad that little real teaching can take place, and little else is relevant until it can be improved. The incidental but often massive improvement shown by no-treatment control groups opens a whole new vista of intervention strategies for the raising of educational standards in disadvantaged neighborhoods.

CHAPTER TWELVE

The Medication of Hyperactive Children in Relation to a Diagnostic-Remedial Method

Hobbits delight in such things,
if they are accurate:
They like to have books filled with things that they already know,
set out fair and square
with no contradictions.
J. R. R. Tolkien

It will no doubt be asked to what extent a diagnostic-remedial approach may be regarded as an alternative to the medication of hyperactive children. This question does not admit of a simple answer, because hyperactivity is a broad term that includes a range of etiologically distinct behavioral conditions. One might say that their only common feature is that the behavioral initiatives of the child meet with adult disapproval and are difficult to control.

There can be no doubt that some hyperactivity arises from the dysfunction of the neural mechanisms that control behavior. It would seem that this dysfunction can affect the behavioral system in two ways. First, it may result in a failure to inhibit or to delay impulses to act, so that the action takes place regardless of the consequences. Second, it may produce a failure to focus attention upon perceptual detail, so that the affected individual appears perceptually handicapped. So-called stimulant drugs help to correct both varieties of dysfunction, but a much greater dosage is probably required for the first than the second, and there is a danger that hyperactive children referred for treatment because they are disruptive may be given dosages that impair their learning. Our chief problem, however, is that by no means all the adult-disapproved, hard-to-control behavior that comes under the general rubric of hyperactivity is caused by neural dysfunction. Marwit and Stenner (1972) have made a distinction between that which is organic and constitutional and that which is learned, to wit, "a life-style developed by the child to cope with his environment." Pursuing this distinction, Murray (1976) notes that the child whose hyperactivity is psychogenic (learned) may show a lack of goal-directed behavior but is capable of concentrating upon and completing a task when he wants to do so. He may be literally hyperactive, but is amenable to externally applied control. Moreover, he has the capability to reflect and to plan, even though this may lie unused until evoked by a behavior-modification or other conditioning procedure.

Failure to recognize the psychogenic origin of much hyperactivity may lead to the unnecessary drugging of certain categories of children. In some subcultures and ethnic groups a level of activity is condoned or encouraged that is detrimental to school learning. Attention is drawn elsewhere in this book to the child whose needs for effectiveness are so strong that they override his social judgment and cause him to embark impulsively upon ill-considered projects (see inappropriate learning style P in Chapter Ten). Children of this type incur disapproval by insisting on doing things their own way, and tire and annoy adults by their initiatives, as exemplified by the case of Ryan in Dr. O'Neill's contribution. Despite the Ross's dedication of their book on hyperactivity to his nanny, the young Winston Churchill appears to have been a child of this sort. He was by no means an "organic" hyperactive, as witness his capacity for absorption in military games, but he was certainly one of the abnormally high-effectiveness type, with the telltale propensity for ill-considered action. The same applies to Napoleon. The mind boggles to think how history and the advance of civilization may be tampered with if the budding geniuses of the next generation are reduced to mediocrity by medication.

The risks involved in the indiscriminate drug treatment of all children diagnosed as hyperactive become all the more serious in view of possibility that where there is no neural basis for the condition, the drugs used may impair learning ability or produce behavior disturbance. Swanson and Kinsbourne (1976) found that the non-hyperactive control children in their experiment made an average of 38 errors while on medication, compared to 28 on the placebo; however, the difference fell just below the level of statistical significance. Nevertheless, this finding indicates that the learning even of some of the children diagnosed as hyperactive will be impaired by drugs.

There is also evidence that medication may produce behavioral and other changes in some hyperactive children that are no less serious than the original condition, and indeed in a sense may be more dangerous because they are likely to be tolerated by adults as the lesser of two evils. Hoffman et al. (1974) reported that, of the 31 children in their study for whom complete data were obtained, nine showed symptoms of hypoactivity, which included lethargy, drowsiness, being subdued or depressed, and appearing dazed or "in a fog." Two showed irritability and moodiness, two had headaches, five suffered from insomnia, and no less than two-thirds of the sample showed a weight loss. The authors of this study were not seeking evidence against drug use; on the contrary, they congratulated themselves that they had confirmed the efficacy of methylphenidate for the treatment of hyperkinesis. They even play down the above changes as side effects that they regard as benign. This assessment may be valid for the temporary use of a drug to treat some critical condition, but, as shown by research findings quoted below, an important feature of medication for the treatment of hyperactivity is that it should be continuous. It is difficult to regard continuous drowsiness, depression, or insomnia as "benign."

It follows that, before prescribing a drug, the clinician has a duty first to make a precise diagnosis of the type of behavior disturbance reported as hyperactive. The pragmatic "try it and see" procedure that Kinsbourne recommends is unrealistic. The process of trial and error must always be a lengthy one, depending upon systematic observation and reporting by teachers and parents, and close liaison between the teacher and the physician. Such liaison is haphazard at present: Weithorn and Ross (1975) found that in only 57% of the cases they surveyed was there any contact between teacher and physician. The alternative would be successive testings of the child's learning ability at varying dosage levels. Such a procedure would be lengthy, and require a trained tester. Moreover, after a few months the process may have to be gone over again because in a good proportion of cases the dosage needs to be increased (Safer and Allen, 1976). In short, considering the above difficulties and the limitations of present professional resources, accurate medication is seldom likely to be attained.

There is a more fundamental objection to the try-it-and-see criterion for medication, even with children in whom it produces an improvement in learning capacity. Just because a child's learning improves in the drug state, it does not imply that he could not have been taught to learn naturally. Dysfunction leading to lack of control is relative. Even a drunk can manage to take care of himself in crossing a street or getting on or off a bus. We can never know what resources of attention and control a child may have until we explore them in a conditioning or other training program. With some children progress is undoubtedly very slow, but this is surely better than freezing the development of their learning skills indefinitely, which, as is argued below, is the most probable effect of long-term medication.

An experiment in the treatment of hyperactivity (Ayllon et al., 1975) illustrates the kinds of uncertainty with which we are faced. The learning of the three children concerned was tested under four conditions: 1) with medication, 2) without medication and with no reinforcement of academic work, 3) without medication but with reinforcement of work at mathematics, and 4) without medication but with reinforcement of work at both mathematics and reading. All three children were chosen because they displayed a noisy, disruptive, restless type of hyperactivity. The medication reduced this behavior to the 24% level, and, when it was discontinued, the level doubled or trebled. When, however, academic performance was reinforced, the hyperactivity level fell to 20%— that is to say, it was somewhat more effective than the medication in controlling the undesirable behavior. Even more significant, when the medication was discontinued and academic performance reinforced, the percentage of correct answers in mathematics and reading rose from 12 to 85%. One explanation of this finding is that the dosage used to control the children's behavior was far in excess of that which might have improved their learning—a consideration that becomes serious when it is appreciated that the level of dosage is more likely to be adjusted to teachers' and parents' reports of behavior than to measures of learning.

Ayllon and his co-workers claim, as a finding of the above experiment, that, "The academic gains produced contrast dramatically with the lack of academic progress shown by these children on medication." It might be objected that they were not 'true' organic hyperactives anyway, but just unruly children. This is unlikely, because the drug significantly reduced their activity level. The upshot is that many other children displaying the same sorts of behavior and placed on medication may have their learning similarly impaired. It is most likely that their hyperactivity arose from a combination of neural dysfunction and lack of discipline. If this were so, their learning would still have improved with a try-it-and-see administration of the drug—and thus meet Kinsbourne's pragmatic criterion—even though they could have learned to control their behavior and could have been trained to adopt useful learning strategies without it.

A further finding by Ayllon and his co-workers should cause us to reflect upon the nature of the training program. When the reinforcement was discontinued, the hyperactivity of all three children immediately increased to a high level. It even happened that hyperactivity was suppressed when mathematical performance was reinforced, but so long as reading performance was not also reinforced it remained at a high level during the reading periods. Thus, in the use of formal behavior modification we have to guard against reliance on artificial external reinforcements that are effective only so long as they are in operation. If we use behavior modification it must be in conjunction with a type of learning that is attractive and therefore reinforcing in itself. In the Ayllon experiment the children found that they had to desist from their hyperactivity in order to perform the tasks that gained them the tokens. Ideally, they should control their hyperactivity spontaneously because they enjoy the task and want to perform it for its own sake.

There is further evidence of the way medication acts that must make us explore the possibility of alternatives. This is to the effect that what is learned in the drug state is not transferred to the non-drug state. The most recent investigation of this issue, that by Swanson and Kinsbourne (1976) referred to above, was methodologically more sophisticated than previous studies in that the investigators chose as their experimental hyperactive group only those children whose learning was shown to improve in the drug state. When both the learning and the testing took place under medication, there was a considerable improvement in performance. However, 27.8% more errors occurred on material learned on medication but tested in the natural state than on material learned and tested in the natural state throughout. In short, not only is there a failure to transfer the learning to the natural state, but hyperactive children who have intermittent medication do worse than if they had none at all. Swanson and Kinsbourne consequently advocate the constant use of medication. One has to ask "For how long?" Kinsbourne takes the view that medication must be continued until such time, if ever, as the child achieves normal control of his mental processes. In this event, he argues, the learning achieved in the drug state will be transferable, because all the drug does is allow the hyperactive child to use the same strategies that make possible good learning in the natural state. If, however, the child, because of his being kept constantly under medication, never has an opportunity to practice these strategies, we have to ask how he can ever acquire them naturally or benefit from a program of training in their use. Surely this is like expecting an alcoholic to adapt metabolically to abstinence while continuing to take his full quota of liquor! Even if the withdrawal of the medication is phased, we can have no assurance that the child will acquire good learning strategies spontaneously. Most hyperactive children have learned to obtain gratification from their style of behavior in the form of pleasure at being the center of attention and disturbance. There is no reason why they should renounce this spontaneously. If a child is already under medication, a phased withdrawal would no doubt be indicated; however, it would need to be accompanied by an equally carefully phased program of training in good learning strategies.

Considering all these uncertainties, and the possibility that medication may hinder the learning of some children diagnosed as hyperactive and act only as a palliative with others, we have a responsibility to explore alternative means of helping hyperactive children to control their behavior and to acquire good learning skills. Because learning gains made under medication are restricted to the drug state, it is doubtful if there is any justification for its use in order to improve learning as such. Direct training in the use of the learning skills of attention and reflectivity, however modest or slow, is, in the long run, more effective than the achievement of drug-dependent gains in the learning of specific material.

In the five years of the development of the Flying Start program at the University of Guelph, during which some 250 kindergarten pupils and a fair number of older children were referred from the school systems, we never had to resort to drugs in the remediation of those of hyperactive temperament. Whereas we made little progress with a small number of children exhibiting other types of dysfunction and psychopathology, over the course of a year all the hyperactive children yielded to treatment in that they learned to fit in, without disruption, in the activities of a group and became good learners. Sometimes behavior-modification techniques had to be used, notably to train them to work well in a group and to attend under a simulation of classroom conditions. Meichenbaum and Goodman (1971) trained children to delay their responses by teaching them to verbalize, first openly and then to themselves, what they were trying to do. Ross and Ross (1976) point to the need for long-term intervention experiments in the training of hyperactive children. Such experiments will be difficult so long as medication remains the rule. There is certainly no justification for Kinsbourne's claim that behavioral forms of treatment do not work. Few have been tried. Owing to the reluctance of behavior modifiers to recognize individual differences of temperament in children, we are still only just beginning to explore their possibilities.

Drugs may sometimes have to be used to control a child's behavior because of the stresses that extreme hyperactivity can impose upon parents and teachers, but even in such cases the possibility of direct control of the behavior should be explored. The exploration should include a study of the discipline used by the adults in charge of the child. Many children have never been in a social situation where they need to control their behavior, and react vigorously against attempts to discipline them. Others have learned to resist by counter-aggressiveness. It is natural that they will try the same tactics in school.

In order to break free from the social binds that have led to indiscriminate drug use on the American continent, nothing less than the establishment of formal regulatory procedures is likely to be of avail. These might be made the responsibility of periodic review conferences that would require evidence of the failure of all other methods. As these alternative methods are developed and become known, my prediction is that only the very exceptional child would qualify for drug treatment, and then as a last resort.

If, as a result of the failure of the remedial reconditioning program, it seems likely that the child's hyperactivity is attributable to neural dysfunction, an expert medical search for its cause should be carried out along the lines developed by Walker (1975). He points out that the use of stimulants merely masks the symptoms and directs attention away from the true causes. The ease with which medication can be prescribed and administered makes it popular as a form of treatment. A practical difficulty in the adoption of Walker's approach to diagnosis is the time it takes. There are not enough pediatricians available to examine all the children reported as hyperactive. This is another reason for an earlier stage in the diagnostic process that would explore the extent to which the child can be trained to control his behavior and to use an appropriate learning style. Only for the few in whom some neural dysfunction was apparent would a Walker-type examination and medication be applicable.

CHAPTER THIRTEEN

Summary
of
Theory and Practice

Effect your meaning.
Then stop.
Confucius

This book offers an integrated diagnostic-remedial method, in contrast to the orthodox procedures of assessing and remediating in separate stages. The traditional procedure was founded on the theoretical assumption of relatively fixed abilities and disabilities. It followed that these had only to be ascertained by formal tests and a prescription for the treatment emerged. If a mental test indicated that a child had a low IQ, he would be exposed to a curriculum thought to be appropriate to his low potential. However, once it is realized that the concept of a "potential" is developmentally meaningless and that the IQ is as much a measure of attainment, albeit over a wider range of function, as are assessments of reading and arithmetic skills (Pidgeon, 1970), the effect of such a placement is to say "This is where the child is, and this is where he stays."

A DEVELOPMENTAL ALTERNATIVE TO "INTELLIGENCE" FOR THE EXPLANATION OF MENTAL DIFFERENCES

Current thinking regarding "intelligence" is in a state of flux. The notion that there is some essential quality of mentation that is reflected in the IQ is still subscribed to by eminent psychologists both in America and in Britain, just as, in the 19th century, respectable and productive geologists clung to the notion of a once-and-for-all divine Creation, even in the face of mounting evidence against it (Gillespie, 1951). It is a comforting bedrock concept that absolves its adherents from further questioning and saves them the discomfort of uncertainty. It is a something-or-other felt to exist simply for lack of any other explanation. As such, it has low status in the world of knowledge. Analogous entities were invented by the thinkers of prescientific cultures to explain all natural phenomena—primitive man believed in witches and spirits, sophisticated philosophers talked of life principles and absolute truths. Once phenomena began to be understood by the building of explanations based on the observed regularities of nature, the placing of responsibility upon some unverifiable agency, construct, or principle became unnecessary, and was seen as contrary to the method of science. Psychology has been the last branch of knowledge to sweep this prescientific animism out of its attics. Indeed, until we put forward a theory to explain mental differences other than by postulating a construct called intelligence, many psychologists will retain the concept as a means of filling the hiatus, even though they are uneasy with it.

In Chapter Three I indicated that an alternative explanation is emerging in the thinking of several leading psychologists, and I have proposed a motivational complement (Stott, 1966) to this explanation. This theory postulates an equipment of basic cognitive mechanisms, namely those of association, selection of relevant percepts by some kind of filtering or appraisal, generalization of information into concepts, storage, and retrieval. Traditional intelligence theory accounts for individual differences by assuming that these basic processes vary in quality and efficiency. It completely neglects the issue of whether the mental organization responsible for them is used or not—whether, by use, it has grown more efficient, or, by non-use, has never developed. Not only, in a mental test, is non-use equated with inability; over a period, non-development amounts to inability.

Because this issue is central to the developmental theory of mental differences, it deserves amplification. In order to solve any problem at beyond the level of trial and error an individual needs to draw on his previous knowledge. He has to know what to expect if he makes a certain choice. This means that he must previously have put together a number of observations and perceived a certain predictive regularity in them. We call these working models of the outside world concepts. In short, every problem-solving act depends upon a certain level of concept development within the sphere in which the individual is operating. Thus, any mental capability depends upon the previous occurrence of a large amount of thinking. It stands to reason, therefore, that the critical variable is that of occurrence or non-occurrence. Beside this, variations in the quality of the process are probably unimportant, especially since the activation of a neural connection is an all-or-none electrical event. Naturally provision has to be made for cases of dysfunction attributable to damage or maldevelopment of brain tissues or exposure to a noxious metabolic environment. Nevertheless, while such pathological conditions account for much mental retardation and the well-known hump at the lower end of a frequency-distribution of IQs, they do not explain variations in mental development above that level.

Next we have to explain what determines this critical variable of occurrence or non-occurrence—in other words, what motivates the brain to be active and thereby to develop its capabilities. It is obvious that a child with strong exploratory tendencies, that is to say, who is determined to find out about things, will acquire a much larger stock of information than the incurious child. The child who insists upon understanding and who ponders unsolved problems is going to advance much more quickly in problem-solving skills than the unreflective child or the child who is frightened by what is complex or strange. Similarly, those who take pleasure in observing fine differences and less obvious similarities, and those who take a pride in attempting difficult tasks by themselves, will advance more than the mentally inert. All the above differences in motivation can be summed up by saying that children have varying needs for competence and effectiveness (Stott, 1961; Stott and Albin, 1975; Stott, Williams, and Sharp, 1976). Some children with low effectiveness-needs are content to shun any issue that carries a risk of failure or frustration. Those with high effectiveness-needs refuse to be defeated, and work at the problem until they have solved it.

Variations in effectiveness-motivation are seen in practical form in certain temperamental differences that affect learning. The unforthcoming child, defined as one in whom the effectiveness-need is deficient or in a state of dysfunction (Stott, Marston, and Neill, 1975), fails to learn because he is frightened of anything new or apparently difficult, and because he does not have the determination to overcome his fears. He is content to operate at a very low level of competence. This type of child is easily recognizable, and is frequently found in retarded settings.

Children with abnormally strong and insistent effectiveness-needs can also become handicapped in their mental development. References have been made in the text to those children whose excessive demands for independence induce them to spurn what other people can teach them. They place themselves at a disadvantage because no individual can, by his own experience, rediscover the accumulated knowledge of his culture. High effectiveness-needs may in addition induce some children to try to get the answer to a problem too quickly. Such impulsivity is often diagnosed as hyperactivity.

ENVIRONMENTAL FACTORS
IN MENTAL DEVELOPMENT AND LEARNING

There are also important factors outside the child that help to determine the development of his mental capabilities. The richness of his home environment will determine the extent to which he has the kinds of perceptual experience and develops the kinds of concepts that will be useful to him in our educational system. Probably even more important are the encouragement and stimulation of different sorts of mental development provided by his culture. With his inclination to make discriminations and to grasp relationships (an aspect of dealing effectively with his world), a child will often take pride in observing something that someone else has missed or in contradicting someone. In many traditional cultures such behavior would be punished as an offense against the established seniority rule. Where people have had to live in a very confined space, such as the tepee of the North American Indian, the avoidance of every sort of irritation was of paramount importance, and questioning or argumentativeness was discouraged. On the other hand, if children are given free rein to argue and catch other people out, they have open to them an area of effectiveness that "sharpens their wits." Some years ago I heard through an open window the following conversation between two girls, (ages about 7 and 9):

> Girl A (the younger): "Mummy forbidded you to do that."
> Girl B: "'Forbidded!' You don't know the right word."
> Girl A: "Mummy forbode you to do that."

The fact that the older girl let the second version pass is neither here nor there. The two girls were interacting in a way calculated to advance their linguistic development.

Similarly, some cultures allow and admire wit-sharpening forms of effectiveness, while others punish them. In some cultures the effectiveness of children is channeled into academic attainment; in others physical dominance carries the highest prestige, and fathers transmit the model by praising the juvenile aggressiveness of their sons and sparring with them in mock battles. In a social group in which no one reads for pleasure, to be a reader is unsociable, and can become the subject of taunts. In the traditional non-academic cultures, the younger generation is discouraged from experimenting in new ways of doing things or from attempting anything problematical—restrictions consistent with the unwritten rule that any potential source of stress should be avoided. The result is that the culture which allows arguing and intellectual assertiveness, and encourages the child to accept the challenge of difficulties confers great advantages on its younger members within our present educational system with regard to knowledge, concept-development, and learning skills. There is no need to postulate ethnic differences in conceptual development. Within its own sphere of wisdom—human interaction—a traditional culture may show a more advanced and explicit conceptual development, embodied in an oral literature of proverbs, than the industrial culture (Bowen, 1964).

Many other influences could be cited that guide the child of the education-conscious family into the forms of attainment and ways of thought of the dominant industrial culture. Such a child is faced with expectations of academic competence that go some way towards overcoming temperamental and other handicaps. In a study of the relationship between temperamental handicaps and reading attainment (Stott, 1959b) unforthcomingness was related to below-average performance, but with a strong social-class differential: in the lowest social group all the unforthcoming children were below average, while the small number of unforthcoming children in the middle-class professional group were all average or forward readers. It is commonplace that children of the latter social group are more likely to receive specific perceptual training, in the form of exposure to pictures, alphabets, and numerals, and to develop skills of attention to visual detail. There is thus no need to attribute the IQ gap between the manual and non-manual worker classes to social-class differences in intelligence. Given the different types of training in the use of cognitive skills, and the differential mental capabilities that develop therefrom, such IQ differences are a foregone conclusion.

SPECIFIC LEARNING DISABILITIES

Many of the objections made above to the concept of intelligence as an explanatory factor also apply to "learning disabilities." When we speak of a child "having a learning disability" we imply some condition or entity analogous to that of a disease. To establish the reality of the cognitive anomaly or anomalies it is necessary to produce a syndrome of symptoms that cannot be accounted for by other means. In Chapter Two I have argued that the most often quoted symptom, left-right reversals, can be more economically explained as a failure of learning in children of impulsive, unreflective temperament, or who have otherwise missed the learning experiences needed to countermand the early-acquired learning to ignore direction. The seriousness with which failure of left-right discrimination is viewed may, if communicated to the child, produce in him an emotionally charged confusion that perpetuates the difficulty. Some young children develop similar blocks about numbers when they are made to feel ashamed of their inability to count (anyone who has learned a foreign language knows the lasting confusion that can arise from the initial learning of a false gender). In my experience, short-term memory deficits are nearly always more properly diagnosed as failure of attention attributable to anxiety-avoidance. Nor must the possibility be overlooked that—just as some children gain a short-term advantage from feigning being dull or retarded—some children may seize upon the uniqueness and attention-drawing advantages of having a "learning disability." When such is diagnosed the child is absolved from facing the challenges of learning. A so-called learning disability may thus be nothing more than a socially conditioned educational neurosis.

In practice the nature of the presumed cognitive anomaly often remains undefined and becomes a mere residual inference. If a child has "normal mental ability" and suffers from no emotional disturbance, yet is performing in school at significantly below the level indicated by his IQ, he is presumed to have "a learning disability" or "specific learning disorder." As Alan Ross (1976) points out, "Since there is no measure of learning potential, such identification is quite difficult." A definition that depends entirely upon the absence of certain characteristics is surely no definition at all. It is an admission of ignorance. A diagnostician forced back upon a residual explanation should at least carry out a thorough search for more tangible reasons for the child's failure to learn.

How often is the child's life history taken from birth and before, the attitudes of his parents to his mental development and learning explored? How often do we ask about the kind of competition (or lack thereof) he has had to face from siblings, his current state of health, the amount of sleep he gets, how many changes of school he has suffered during the critical years for mastering reading, and so on? In my own diagnostic work I have never had to fall back upon a residual diagnosis of specific learning disability. Investigation by discussion with the parents often reveals a common-sense explanation. For example, a naturally active boy whose preference is for sports is told by his father, "Never mind, son, I had trouble with reading when I was at school." In such a case a teacher or psychologist, unaware that the child is proudly modeling himself upon his father in scorning reading, could easily be nonplussed and tempted to resort to the fashionable diagnosis of a learning disability.

Perhaps the weakest link in the residual diagnosis of a learning disability is that of the exclusion of "emotional disturbance." (This in itself is a misleading euphemism for behavior disturbance. Many obviously behavior-disturbed hyperactive children are not in the least emotionally disturbed; it is those who have to care for them who may become such.) We have to ask, again, how often is a systematic assessment made of a child's behavioral stability? If a child is exceedingly hyperactive, or hostile or withdrawn, no doubt an informal report from teacher or parent will serve to direct attention to the disturbance, but many less obtrusive forms of disturbance may be missed. An impulsivity that is mild enough in everyday life and hardly noticed in some cultures because it is typical of the lifestyle may nonetheless generate a faulty style of learning and hence be responsible for learning failure. An unforthcomingness seen merely as unventuresomeness and shyness may not be considered "emotional disturbance," yet it may lead to a retreat from the challenges of learning. Likewise, depression caused by a health problem, lack of sleep, or disturbed home conditions may be overlooked, although it destroys the child's motivation to learn. Finally, there are those specific anxieties arising from unfortunate learning experiences that produce blockage of the cognitive processes without affecting the child's general social adjustment. An elementary diagnostic precaution, seldom taken, because most professional psychologists have not yet learned to think in such terms, is to obtain from the teacher an assessment of the child's learning style, that is to say, exactly how he sets about learning tasks. This bases the diagnosis upon observable behavioral indications that represent something positive rather than hypothetical.

Alan Ross has made a notable advance in this direction by defining learning disability as a failure to sustain selective attention. He attributes this failure to a "developmental lag." In the literal and most parsimonious interpretation of the term, it obviously is just that; however, the term carries the imputation of anomaly. If this is what Ross means to imply, we are thrown back upon the hypothesis of some unidentified organic maldevelopment or dysfunction. A diagnostic-teaching approach, such as Ross himself advocates, reveals that there are many reasons why children may suffer from an inability to maintain selective attention. It may be because they are tired or hungry, or have never been trained to give selective attention to the things that we select for them, or are avoiding learning because it is a source of tension. There is thus no justification for treating this particular inability as if it were a disease entity. Neither is there any reason for honoring only inattentive children with the prestigious label of learning disability. What about those who suffer from a developmental lag in the form of lack of confidence?

We may further ask, if the rationale of a concept has been destroyed, what point there is in trying to perpetuate its name with new hypotheses. This is to chase a will-o'-the-wisp, just as psychologists for two generations have been chasing the will-o'-the-wisp of intelligence. In effect, many leading authorities in this field are no longer so confident as heretofore in differentiating learning disabilities from other categories of learning failure. There is an obvious temptation to promote the term for political reasons, notably as a means of getting government support for programs. However, this tactic can rebound upon those who accept a general responsibility for the hard-to-teach child. The vagueness of the term is likely to lead, and is now leading, to official scepticism; and the large number of children who are failing to learn but do not answer to the rubric risk are being overlooked and educationally neglected. It is best, while there is still time, for us and the community organizations committed to the term "learning disabilities" to substitute for it the broader term "learning difficulties." That many children suffer from learning difficulties is a fact, and it is they who, without political differentiation, should be our educational concern.

In a book designed primarily to describe a diagnostic-remedial program at a practical level, these theoretical polemics against the concepts of intelligence and learning disabilities may seem to be out of place, but this is not so. False theories lead to false practices. The inappropriateness of our present practices in the field of learning difficulties has led to a state of uncertainty, discouragement, and frustration—and above all to a failure to develop comprehensive remedial programs for all hard-to-teach children.

THE DIAGNOSTIC-REMEDIAL STRATEGY

It is appropriate here to summarize the alternative practice that follows from the new theory. The first stage of diagnosis is to discover in what way the child has failed to use, and hence to develop, his cognitive capabilities. This should include their aberrant use, as in the case of retardates and other slow-learning children, who exercise considerable ingenuity in deriving advantage from incompetence. A study of the child's learning and coping styles should be made even if it is apparent that the child suffers from cognitive damage or maldevelopment. The natural tendency of such children is to play a more retarded role than they need in order to escape pressures and enjoy the advantages of dependence. Few retardates operate mentally to the full extent of their capabilities (Stott, 1977). This stage of the investigation does not aim to place the child in a particular category of handicap, that is, to give him a label. It merely aims to achieve an understanding of his faulty learning habits.

The second stage of the diagnosis involves work with the child in a remedial program, a primary objective of which is to correct the faulty learning habits. A new diagnostic dimension then becomes available to us—the speed with which the child learns how to learn. If the original faults of learning style are mainly attributable to lack of previous training in the learning skills required for progress in school, or the perpetuation of ways of coping with developmental handicaps that have since disappeared, we may expect the improvement to be rapid. In this case the child has the necessary flexibility in his repertoire of cognitive styles, but the appropriate styles have lain dormant.

Naturally, the value of this exploration of improvability and flexibility depends upon the use of a remedial technology that will induce the child to bring his capabilities into play. Some remedial methods do the opposite: for example, direct teaching on a one-to-one basis is fraught with danger, since the child is cornered into having to respond to the adult's questioning. If the pressure is greater than he can stand, he will resort to an avoidance strategy. This may be a retreat into a defensive position of dullness (which becomes all the more accepted in view of our readiness to diagnose low intelligence), or the play-acting of tiredness and distractibility, or an unconscious blockage of the cognitive processes of attention and recall, seen as a fading of concentration and so-called short-term memory deficit. The reshaping of the child's learning style requires carefully planned schedules of conditioning. Any use by the child of productive mental strategies, such as a modicum of attention, taking a moment to think, a willingness to attempt a problem, however simple, should be rewarded by success. The success should be of a type that children seek naturally in their play and other everyday activities, namely an enhancement of their feelings of effectiveness. The achievement should be seen by the child as the immediate result of his own effort. The teacher may judiciously further reinforce by praise, but the main reinforcement should arise from the exercise of competence within the activity itself. Only in this way will the child acquire learning skills that are transferable because they consist of a generally effective method for solving problems. A child constantly reinforced with approval may learn nothing more than strategies for getting the right answers by picking up cues from the adult. The chosen remedial activities should be so loaded with effectiveness-enhancing opportunities that the child finds them as enjoyable as spontaneous play. This applies particularly to children who have become conditioned by failure, pressure, and disgrace to regard all learning activities as unrewarding and aversive.

If limits of improvability are reached that fall short of full remediation, a systematic search for the ongoing handicap, involving specialized test instruments, is indicated. Nevertheless, the results of the tests should still be regarded as a measure of the child's capabilities in the area at the time of testing. The extent to which a child can use his motor and other physical abilities will depend, just as his learning does, upon his ability to attend to the physical situation, to control his impulsivity, and to acquire the confidence to attempt tasks. Ideally all such testing should also aim to measure the critical dimension of improvability through a program of alternate testing and training. The golden rule is that diagnosis must remain a continuous monitoring of the child's developing capabilities, rather than a one-shot "assessment." In addition, the conditions diagnosed and treated should be observable and empirically defined rather than residual constructs, the only value of which has been to provide the psychologist and special educator with a professional mystique.

Nevertheless, the diagnostic-remedial method I have proposed is a teaching procedure as much as, or more than, it is a clinical procedure. As teachers become more sophisticated in observing children's shortcomings in terms of faults of learning strategy, there will be less need for psychological intervention, and as teachers learn to create conditions for learning in their pupils that are realistic both in terms of the nature of the learning process and the wide variety of individual temperament and background, fewer hard-to-teach children will be produced.

At the present time, teaching is an inexcusably haphazard business. It is the outcome of methods evolved for different sorts of pupils in different cultural settings, methods that are passed down from generation to generation in defiance of any pedagogy that might have been taught in colleges. The child is at the mercy of the individual style of his teacher. If that style is good, he thrives; a good teacher for a single year can enhance a child's mental development for life. If his teacher's style is poor, or ill-suited to the child's needs, the result may be a discouragement and rejection that restricts a child's mental development for life.

The first measures in the prevention of learning failure should consequently be directed toward a review of our methods of teaching children—and of teaching teachers. We need to develop a body of professional knowledge and skills that includes an understanding of the processes of learning that is not pedantically derived from a mechanistic stimulus-response theory but that takes into account the social and motivational conditions in which effective learning takes place. In Chapter Eight, following the lead of Gagné, I have proposed ten conditions for learning that may serve as a starting point for the discussion of criteria by which teachers may assess their teaching.

In these days, when individual freedoms are paramount, to objectify the teaching process by explicit criteria may appear to depersonalize it. There is no such antithesis. We expect our family doctor not only to be human but also to be correct. The exercise of a technology based upon a body of knowledge is the mark of a profession. A generation of children and their parents have a right to expect that whatever freedom a teacher may claim in the exercise of a personal style, that style shall be consonant with good technique.

APPENDIX A

The Guide to The Child's Learning Skills

The checklist of styles of coping with learning situations, as reproduced in this appendix, was built up over some five years through the observation of successive groups of young children identified by their teachers as likely to have continuing learning difficulties. It takes the form of a series of fifteen[1] main headings, which are not scored but which serve to direct the teacher to the more detailed descriptions beneath them. The latter are graded by presumed severity on a scoring scale of 0 to 3. Each score has meaning only for the particular fault of learning style to which it refers, and as the basis for a profile, a form for which is also reproduced. It is not intended that the scores for all styles should be added to produce a total score. A very severe single fault, while unlikely, may result in complete incapacity within the child's contemporary academic setting, yet only contribute 3 points, while a number of moderate faults scored as 1 may contribute a larger total. For certain purposes, however, it would be permissible to group the scores for allied styles in order to obtain measures of overreacting or underreacting types of response, or as a general screening for hyperactivity. In the latter case it would be advisable to subsequently break down the assessment into the various faulty learning strategies that come under the general rubric of hyperactivity.

---

[1] Only fourteen of these are descriptions of faulty learning styles in the strict sense of the term. Section O really records the teacher's impression that the child does not have the cognitive grasp to be aware of what the task calls for. This may or may not be the case, but the teacher has to be given the opportunity to report this impression. Its significance should be assessed in relation to the other descriptions marked.

The Guide to the Child's Learning Skills (GCLS) records contemporary behaviors that have been found to be typical of children who meet with difficulties in their school learning. It does not diagnose handicaps as such, i.e., the underlying causes of the difficulties. These latter are of course reflected in some kind of faulty learning or problem-solving procedure. However, very different handicaps or disadvantages, operating either within or upon a child, may produce similar faults of strategy.

A record of the behavior and attitudes observed in the child when faced with a learning task is thus only the first stage, or baseline, of diagnosis. As explained in the main text, it is followed by an exploration of the child's ability to overcome his faulty learning habits and to develop a capability for learning. This takes the form of a program of diagnostic teaching. The GCLS can be reused at its conclusion as a measure of progress. No good or normal alternatives are provided, because the Guide is intended to be used only for the assessment of children referred as educationally high-risk or identified as likely to be such by the use of the *Preliminary Screening* checklist, which forms the last page of this appendix.

The prime purpose of the Preliminary Screening form is to obviate the necessity, in an identification procedure, of completing the full GCLS for every child in a class, which, besides being burdensome, would try the teacher's resources of concentration.

Preliminary Screening forms for a class of thirty can be completed in an hour. Only those children for whom a number of questions are marked adversely (i.e., to the effect that the description of a *good* style doesn't apply) would be singled out for a more detailed recording of their learning behavior. The cut-off point for an adverse score has to be decided upon in the light of the cultural and socioeconomic features of the area served by the school and by the resources of remediation available. Because of the great variations in learning skills observed in different cultural and socioeconomic groups it will be hardly feasible to establish general norms. This is best done within the population surveyed.

The premise that the faulty learning styles identified in the GCLS are responsible for continuing learning failure is being investigated in follow-up studies over one or more years, using attainment in reading and arithmetic as the dependent variables. Details of the designs of these studies, and their eventual findings, will be supplied by the author on request.

Note: Although the GCLS is formally copyrighted, a license to reproduce it for purposes of research or assessment will be granted to qualified persons or appropriate institutions for a nominal annual fee (to cover the costs of supplying copies for reproduction). In the United Kingdom interested persons should apply to the Centre on Educational Disadvantage, 11 Anson Road, Manchester M14 5BY. Others should apply direct to the author, Dr. D. H. Stott, 30 Colborn Street, Guelph, Ontario, N1G 2M5.

GUIDE TO THE
CHILD'S LEARNING SKILLS

A schedule for the systematic observation of learning behavior, compiled by D. H. Stott, Ph.D.

Name of child_____ Date of birth_____

Teacher completing Guide_____

School_____

Class_____Type of class_____

Date_____ Sex of child_____

Identification of Poor Learning Habits

Before completing this section of the Guide it is best to read it through with the child in mind and then put it aside for a week. This will give you time to study how the child copes with learning in the light of the questions asked.

When you do complete this section, first read the statements printed in capitals (they are marked A, B, C, etc.). If any applies to the child, read the three statements below it and put a mark against whichever one of them (Somewhat, Definite, Severe) most closely describes his attitude to learning. You may mark as many of the sections as you consider fit the child.

(A) **HE/SHE IS AFRAID TO BEGIN OR TO COMMIT HIMSELF TO ANSWER**

(28)

SOMEWHAT: Is afraid of a new task, inclined to make hesitant, nervous guesses.   ☐ 1

DEFINITE: You have to coax every answer out of him; you almost have to tell him before he will commit himself.   ☐ 2

SEVERE: You can hardly get an answer out of of him. Very frightened of anything new or supposedly difficult.   ☐ 3

(B) **DULL OR BRIGHT AS IT PLEASES HIM TO BE**

(29)

SOMEWHAT: Is very slow when expected to give an answer, but can be sensible in everyday life.   ☐ 1

DEFINITE: The more individual help you give him the more stupid he becomes, but he is by no means so stupid in real life.   ☐ 2

SEVERE: Adopts an attitude of extreme help-lessness and dependence, but close observation shows that he arranges things to his liking.   ☐ 3

(C) **HE/SHE HAS SOLITARY, PECULIAR WAYS OF USING LEARNING OR PLAY MATERIALS**

(30)

SOMEWHAT: Follows some solitary procedure that seldom varies.   ☐ 1

DEFINITE: Insists, despite coaxing, upon follow-ing his own peculiar procedure in exactly the same way each time and refuses to vary it.   ☐ 2

SEVERE: Reacts against the materials, or against anything novel, as an interference with his own private world.   ☐ 3

(D) **HE/SHE ACTS WITHOUT TAKING TIME TO LOOK OR TO WORK THINGS OUT**

(31)

SOMEWHAT: Often "doesn't use his eyes" and answers without thinking.   ☐ 1

DEFINITE: Will guess lightheartedly unless point-edly reminded to take time to think.   ☐ 2

SEVERE: *Never* takes time to look properly or to think out an answer.   ☐ 3

(E)   HE/SHE IS EASILY DISTRACTED

(32)

SOMEWHAT: Allows himself to be distracted to the extent that he doesn't get on with the job in hand.   ☐ 1

DEFINITE: Creates frequent distractions for himself and others; behaves in a silly clowning way or creates disturbances.   ☐ 2

SEVERE: Flits rapidly from one momentary interest to another without ever doing anything productive.   3

(F)   HE/SHE IS OVER-ACTIVE AND FIDGETY

(33)

SOMEWHAT: Seems to find sitting still uncomfortable, nearly always moving some part of his body.   ☐ 1

DEFINITE: -   Fidgets and squirms, constantly changes his position or wanders around.   ☐ 2

SEVERE: Won't keep his seat, runs around the room or charges off unless closely watched.   ☐ 3

(G)   HE/SHE CAN AT TIMES HAVE UNPREDICTABLE OUTBURSTS

(34)

SOMEWHAT: Has been known occasionally to have a wild outburst for no particular reason.   ☐ 1

DEFINITE: Works well at times and is not constantly hyperactive, but, without warning, shouts out, jostles or strikes other children, or upsets the learning materials.   ☐ 2

SEVERE: Has frequent violent outbursts, such as attacking adults or other children or running off without apparent reason.   ☐ 3

(H)   HE/SHE LOOKS FOR WAYS OF EVADING LEARNING TASKS

(35)

SOMEWHAT: Shies off the task at first or soon says he doesn't want to do any more, but can be persuaded.   ☐ 1

DEFINITE: Seeks excuses to get away from the task; complains of being tired or bored.   ☐ 2

SEVERE: Objects strongly when faced with any task.   ☐ 3

(J) **HE/SHE SETS ABOUT TASKS AS IF HE DOESN'T CARE**

(36)

SOMEWHAT:	Has low standards and doesn't try very hard.	□ 1
DEFINITE:	Adopts a don't care attitude toward success or failure.	□ 2
SEVERE:	Seems to take a pride in giving answers that he knows must be wrong just to show he doesn't care.	□ 3

(K) **HE/SHE SUFFERS AT TIMES (OR CONSTANTLY) FROM A LACK OF ENERGY**

(37)

SOMEWHAT:	Sometimes has a lazy mood, and doesn't notice or think things out.	□ 1
DEFINITE:	It is hard to stir him to take an interest or to make any effort.	□ 2
SEVERE:	Is permanently so lethargic and tired that he hardly accomplishes anything.	□ 3

(L) **HE/SHE RELIES ON PERSONAL CHARM TO AVOID LEARNING**

(38)

SOMEWHAT:	Gets along by appealing ways or helpfulness but tends to avoid work.	1
DEFINITE:	Uses his/her personal charm to get individual help, but makes little effort to learn.	□ 2
SEVERE:	Relies entirely on individual charm and doesn't mind how badly he does or how retarded he appears.	□ 3

(M) **HE/SHE HAS HOSTILE MOODS DURING WHICH HE REFUSES TO WORK**

(39)

SOMEWHAT:	Pouts and refuses to begin at first.	□ 1
DEFINITE:	Gets antagonistic when things go against him or he fails, and threatens to quit.	□ 2
SEVERE:	Shrugs off help angrily, refuses to work or quits the scene.	□ 3

(N) **HE/SHE SEEMS TO TRY TO ATTEND, AND IS NOT HYPERACTIVE OR DISTRACTIBLE, BUT CANNOT CONCENTRATE**

(40)

SOMEWHAT:	Seems to try hard but cannot keep his mind on the task, and gets things wrong that he was getting right.	□ 1

DEFINITE:	As soon as he is asked anything his mind flies off at a tangent.	☐ 2
SEVERE:	Cannot be induced to focus his attention on anything.	☐ 3

(O) HE/SHE DOESN'T SEEM AWARE OF WHAT THE TASK CALLS FOR

41

SOMEWHAT:	Difficult to get him to understand what to do.	☐ 1
DEFINITE:	Attends to the task but doesn't seem aware that something is required of him.	☐ 2
SEVERE:	Disregards the task soon after noticing the materials.	☐ 3

(P) HE/SHE PREFERS HIS OWN WAY OF DOING THINGS, WHICH OFTEN DOESN'T WORK OUT

42

SOMEWHAT:	Is not interested in regular learning acitvities but talks intelligently and finds his own interests.	☐ 1
DEFINITE:	Gets behind because he insists on trying to do things his own way.	☐ 2
SEVERE:	Is creative and imaginative, but is impatient of the routines of learning, so that his achievement is very poor.	☐ 3

GUIDE TO THE
CHILD'S LEARNING SKILLS

A schedule for the systematic observation of learning behavior, compiled by D. H. Stott, Ph.D.

Name of child_____Sex _____ Date of birth_____

Teacher completing Guide_____Date of completing Guide____

School_____

Class_____ Type of class_____

PRELIMINARY SCREENING

Mark the appropriate space against each of the following statements, taking into consideration the child's age.

	Certainly applies	Applies sometimes	Doesn't apply
Shows by his answers that he is giving attention.	(21) 1	2	3
Settles down well at an activity that needs some concentration.	(22) 1	2	3
Copes with something new without getting nervous or upset.	(23) 1	2	3
Is willing to fall in with the general activities of the class.	(24) 1	2	3
Is willing to try on his own.	(25) 1	2	3
Accepts help when he cannot manage a task.	(26) 1	2	3
Is an alert child who enters into activities with interest.	(27) 1	2	3

158

GUIDE TO THE
CHILD'S LEARNING SKILLS
Profile of Faulty Learning Styles

Name of child _____ Boy/Girl _____

Teacher _____ Class _____

Type of class _____ Date of completing Guide _____

Physical handicap _____

Social handicap _____

TYPE OF FAULTY LEARNING STYLE	Punch card column	DEGREE OF SEVERITY (punch card row)		
		1	2	3
A - Afraid to begin or to commit himself	28			
B - Assumes role of dull child	29			
C - Solitary, peculiar ways	30			
D - Impulsive	31			
E - Distractible	32			
F - Over-active and fidgety	33			
G - Unpredictable	34			
H - Ways of evading	35			
J - Doesn't care	36			
K - Lethargy	37			
L - Relies on charm	38			
M - Hostile moods	39			
N - Loss of concentration	40			
O - Seems not aware	41			
P - Insists on own way	42			

The Flying Start
Materials as a
Program of Training
in
Learning Skills

The Flying Start materials consist of a series of gamelike activities, the object of which is to give training in effective learning and problem-solving strategies. They were designed and field-tested with children ages 5–7 years old and the older retarded. However, the items are graduated and have alternative methods of use, so that some of them can be used for the remediation of faulty learning habits irrespective of age. The activities are used in different ways according to the type of faulty learning style identified, but the child works through the whole series of items, whatever his particular faults or deficits. Learning and problem-solving contain three components: the focusing of attention, the processing of the information received through the mind (which also entails allowing time for this to happen), and being willing to tackle a problem. If any of these components is missing, no learning occurs. The tasks of the Flying Start require all three, although in the earliest part of the series only at a very elemental level. Thus, in working through the program, the child gets training in whichever component he has weaknesses. The teacher will vary the emphasis for a particular child according to the type of faulty learning style identified by the Guide to the Child's Learning Skills, or by her observation of the child's learning habits.

The Flying Start is essentially a program of conditioning. The items are designed in such a way that, according to the level at which the child is working, use of the above prerequisites for learning brings success in the task. Lapses into behavior that is unproductive for learning remain unreinforced. The goals of the activities are to give the child feelings of effectiveness and competence. Thus the rewards are built into the activity itself and there is normally no need to supply external reinforcements. The child's learning skills are shaped by observing the results of his own responses. These he can see for himself immediately, or they are signalled to him by his game partner. This self-correcting feature of the materials means that the child is spared the possible anxiety of having to answer to an adult, and that he cannot manipulate the adult to provide the answers for him.

The Flying Start differs from other early-education materials in two further respects. The first is that the pieces that have to be fitted together to form a picture consist of uniform shapes with straight lines at their joining edges, and not of irregular shapes as in traditional jigsaws. The purpose of this is to force the child to exercise visual perception in deciding whether a piece is correctly placed. That is to say, he has to notice whether the piece added is consistent with the rest of the picture. As long as it is possible to use the piece's shape as a criterion, it is tempting to work by a motor trial-and-error. This applies particularly to impulsive children who have never "learned to use their eyes" and to the retarded, who are content with slow and ineffective methods of work. With these children the provision of an irregular shape as a guide to correctness reinforces an unprogressive learning strategy.

Many children show unmistakable pleasure upon perceiving that the piece added makes sense with the rest of the picture (the horse gets legs or the fisherman gets a fish on his rod). It will be recalled that the achievement of recognition and discrimination was mentioned above as one of the sources of effectiveness-motivation. Eleanor Gibson (1969) has drawn attention to a similar motivation: "the need to detect what goes on in the world around us is a strong motive in its own right . . . we are set to discriminate things." The endless delights of recognition and discrimination are essential to the major appeals of the visual arts and of music. These pleasures are experienced by children from infancy. The reinforcement they afford extends their knowledge of the world and stimulates their mental development. Nevertheless, in some children this quest for a refinement and enlargement of their experience is inhibited, either by environmental deprivation or by the handicaps of their own temperament. One of the main training objectives of the Flying Start is to reinstate this powerful intelligence-forming motivation.

The second feature distinguishing the Flying Start from other early-education materials is that color is used only as a sequence-guide to the teacher. The reason for this is that the sensuous appeal of color has such primacy in the mechanisms of recognition that it interferes with the growth of the kinds of discrimination skills that are educationally most valuable. The symbols used in writing and computation are in monochrome. Moreover, a child with low effectiveness-needs may remain content with the satisfaction of a very elemental discrimination between the primary colors and will not advance to the more useful monochrome discrimination unless forced to do so by the nature of the task.

DESCRIPTION OF THE ITEMS OF THE FLYING START

The TWO-PIECE PUZZLES (Figure 1) require merely the joining of the two halves of a boldly drawn picture. They invite the apprehensive or the retarded child to commit himself to a very easy task. It may

Figure 1. The Two- and Four-Piece Puzzles.

Figure 2. The Mail Boxes.

be necessary at first to place the two halves almost touching before the child will muster the confidence to look at the materials and appreciate in them an opportunity for achievement. In such children this readiness to participate represents a critical advance. Once they have made this advance they are usually able to make progress beyond what might be anticipated from their apparent retardation.

The FOUR-PIECE PUZZLES consist of the same pictures cut into four equal rectangles. Familiarity with the subject of the pictures facilitates the maintenance of confidence. Whereas the fitting of four pieces demands more perseverance, once the child grasps their general arrangement he can still achieve a completion very quickly, and so receive rapid reinforcement of his decision to attempt the task.

The MAIL BOXES (Figure 2) require the child to post cards bearing letter symbols in the boxes having the corresponding symbols on their fronts. A child at the receiving side of the box turns the card over and checks the half-picture on its reverse with a half-picture on the floor of the box. If the two halves correspond, he signifies that the posting was correct, thus giving the posting child immediate knowledge of the result of his choice. If the latter relies upon trial and error, he runs a three-to-one risk of being pronounced wrong. Guessing is therefore punished by a "loss of face." On the other hand, the small amount of attention needed to discriminate between the letters is rewarded by success and a consequent feeling of competence. Because the checking child is also continually exercising competence in his role of arbiter, the Mail Boxes have great motivating value.

The MERRY-GO-ROUNDS (Figure 3) were originally designed to overcome the inability of young impulsive children to await their turn in a game. The task consists in building up a circle from eight segments, the half pictures of which are matched at their joining edges; however, each of the two players has alternate segments, so that impatient attempts to build a meaningful circle using only one's own pieces produce no whole pictures.

It was later found that even very hyperactive children who refused to commit themselves to the other materials were attracted by the visually easily grasped circular shape and accepted the challenge to complete it.

The WHAT'S HAPPENING CARDS (Figure 4) give training in studying a picture in order to interpret an event, which requires more sustained attention than the recognition of an image. A second

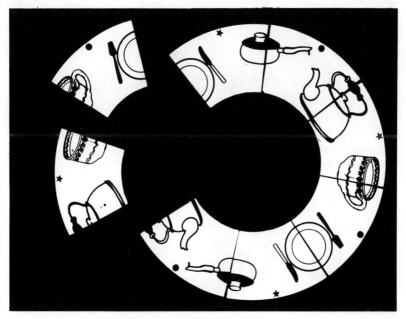

Figure 3. The Merry-go-Rounds.

Figure 4. The What's Happening Cards.

training objective is that of using a methodical approach to a task. The child first places the pictures in the order shown by the numbers on their back, using a number line if necessary. As he turns over each segment in sequence, he finds that it will fit on one end or the other of the strip picture.

The SIX- and EIGHT-PIECE ANIMAL PUZZLES (Figure 5) extend this training in the use of a methodical strategy, involving a delay of

Figure 5. The Six-Piece Animal Puzzle.

response, by the same device. The segments are numbered on their backs in such a way that, joined according to the number sequence, they always have a place for each to fit. If a child impatiently departs from the sequence he makes difficulties for himself.

The MATCHERS (Figure 6) are similar in format to the series of cards designed by Kagan to measure delay of response, except that the subject has to go through three stages of discrimination in order to be sure of choosing the exactly matching card from the row of six. In the figure, if the child goes by only one criterion—that the pirate on the presented card is wearing a hat—he will still stand only one chance in three of making a correct match. If he stops at noting that the pirate also has a peg-leg, he stands a one-in-two chance. Certainty depends upon noting in addition which leg is wooden. Correctness of choice is shown by the tallying of bars on the backs of the cards.

The LEFT-RIGHT cards (Figure 7) were designed to deal with a common perceptual problem in school learning, that of distinguishing the orientation of letters and numerals. It was argued in the main text that this should not be regarded as an indication of anomaly, but rather as evidence that the child has not undergone a special process of supplementary learning. The latter is required in order to countermand the earlier learning that direction may be ignored—and in fact has to be ignored—in the recognition of objects. Pavlov found that the countermanding of old by new learning

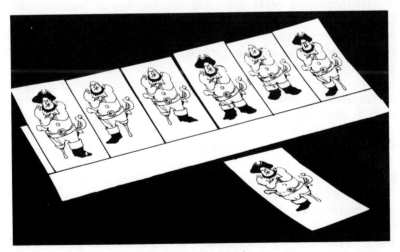

Figure 6. The Matchers.

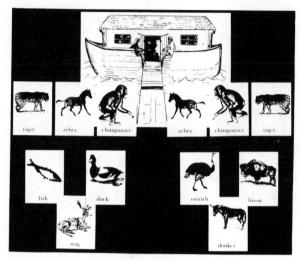

Figure 7. The Left-Right cards.

tends to cause confusion because the old, being more firmly established, fades at a slower rate and crops up again after an interval.
Consequently, learning symbol orientation requires a thoroughgo-
ing reconditioning over a period of time. It is not surprising that
children with poor general learning skills miss out on this process
and continue to show left-right confusions.

In the Flying Start, left-right training begins with the differentiation of b's, d's, p's, and q's in the Mail Boxes. Nearly all the
sets of pictures in the Matchers cards involve left-right discrimination, and two of the later sets specifically require such with letters
and numerals.

In the Left-Right cards, the concept of directional cuing is
developed by successive experiences. In free play with the cards the
child discovers that there are two of each animal, one facing to the
right and the other to the left. When, in the next phase, he has to
line them up to walk into a Noah's Ark, he has to place them so that
they are facing toward, and not away from, the entrance. In the
third phase he learns to connect direction and "sideness" with his
own hands and arms.

The FAMILIES cards (Figure 8) aim to provide a setting for the
spontaneous structuring of experiences into categories. A child or
group of children is given a medley of cards containing pictures of
everyday objects. The natural tendency to structure or classify ob-

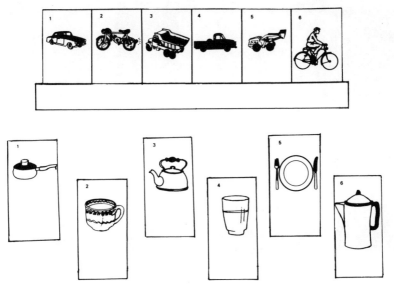

Figure 8. The Families cards.

jects will induce them to sort out the pictures, one child deciding to collect road vehicles, another furniture, a third animals, and so on. The goal of completing a set of six requires innumerable acts of perceptual discrimination and many decisions about whether an object belongs to one category or another.

In the above descriptions of the Flying Start materials only their use with young children or with retarded children at a similar level of development is described. The Flying Start Manual gives more sophisticated games for the more advanced items (Matchers, Left-Right, and Families) in order to extend their use to older children or to retarded adults who require training in productive learning strategies.

REFERENCES

Ausubel, D. P. 1969. Readings in School Learning. Holt, Rinehart, and Winston, New York.

Ayllon, T., Layman, D., and Kandel, H. J. 1975. A behavioral-educational alternative to drug-control of hyperactive children. J. Appl. Behav. Anal. 8:137–146.

Bannatyne, A. 1975. Research design and progress in remediating learning disabilities. J. Learn. Disabil. 8:345–348.

Bateman, B. 1965. An educator's view of a diagnostic approach to learning disorders, Vol. 1. Special Child Publications, Seattle.

Baumeister, A. A., and Muma, J. A. 1975. On defining mental retardation. J. Spec. Educ. 9:293–306.

Beilin, H. 1959. Teachers' and clinicians' attitudes towards the behavior problems of children: A reappraisal. Child Devel. 30:9–25.

Bennett, N. 1976. Teaching styles and pupil progress. London, Open Books.

Berlyne, D. E. 1960. Conflict, Arousal and Curiosity. McGraw Hill, New York.

Blackman, L. S. 1972. Research and the classroom: Mahomet and the Mountain revisited. Except. Child. 39:181–191.

Bowen, E. S. 1964. Return to Laughter, pp. 142–155. Doubleday, Garden City, N.Y.

Bricker, W. A. 1970. Identifying and modifying behavioral deficits. Am. J. Ment. Defic. 75:16–21.

Broman, B. L. 1970. The short attention-span: Fact and myth. Childhood Education, pp. 156–158, Dec. 1970.

Bruner, J. S. 1966. Toward a Theory of Instruction. Belknap Press of Harvard University Press, Cambridge, Mass.

Bruner, J. S. 1968. The course of cognitive growth. In N. S. Endler, L. B. Boulter, and H. Osser (eds.), Contemporary Issues in Developmental Psychology. Holt, Rinehart, and Winston, New York.

Bruner, J. S., Jolly, A., and Sylva, K. 1976. Play: Its role in Development and Evolution. Penguin Books, Harmsworth, Middlesex.

Buckland, P., and Balow, B. 1973. Effect of visual perceptual training on reading achievement. Except. Child. 39:299–308.

Budoff, M. 1974. Measuring learning potential: An alternative to the traditional intelligence test. In G. R. Gredler (ed.), Ethical and Legal Factors in the Practice of School Psychology. State Department of Education, Harrisburg, Pa.

Clarke, A. D. B., and Blakemore, C. B. 1961. Age and perceptual-motor transfer in imbeciles. Brit. J. Psychol. 52:125–131.

Coleman, J. S. 1967. Learning through games. Natl. Educ. Ass. J.

Collins, J. E. 1961. The effects of remedial education. Educational Monographs No. 4. Oliver and Boyd, Edinburgh.

Denny, M. R. 1964. Research in learning and performance. In H. A. Stevens and R. Heber (eds.), Mental Retardation: A Review of Research, pp. 100–136. The University of Chicago Press, Chicago.

171

Deutsch, M. 1963. The disadvantaged child and the learning process. *In* A. H. Passow (ed.), Education in Depressed Areas. Bureau of Publications, Teachers College, Columbia University, New York.

Dunn, L. M. 1968. Special education for the mildly retarded—Is much of it justifiable? Except. Child. 35:5-22.

Endler, N. S., Boulter, L. R., and Osser, H. 1968. Contemporary issues in developmental psychology. Editors' introduction. Holt, Rinehart, and Winston, New York.

Feshbach, S., Adelman, H., and Fuller, W. W. 1974. Early identification of children with high risk of reading failure. J. Learn. Disabil. 7:639-644.

Feuerstein, R. 1968. A dynamic approach to the causation, prevention, and alleviation of retarded performance. *In* H. C. Haywood (ed.), Sociocultural Aspects of Mental Retardation. Appleton-Century-Crofts, New York.

Feuerstein, R. 1978. The Dynamic Assessment of Retarded Performers: The Learning Potential Assessment Device—Theory, Instrumentation, and Techniques. University Park Press, Baltimore. In press.

Forness, S. R., and Esveldt, K. C. 1975. Classroom observation of children with learning and behaviour problems. J. Learn. Disabil. 8:382-385.

Gagné, R. M. 1965. The Conditions of Learning. Holt, Rinehart, and Winston, New York.

Gagné, R. M. 1968. Contributions of learning to human development. Psychol. Rev. 75:177-191.

Garrison, M., and Hammill, D. D. 1971. Who are the retarded? Except. Child. 38:13-20.

Gibson, E. J. 1969. Principles of Perceptual Learning and Development. Appleton-Century-Crofts and Meredith, New York.

Gillespie, C. C. 1951. Genesis and Geology, pp. 200-221. Harvard University Press, Cambridge, Mass.

Glaser, R. 1972. Individuals and learning: The new aptitudes. Educ. Res., June, 1972.

Gordon, I. J. 1973. On early learning: The modifiability of human potential. *In* P. Satz and J. J. Ross (eds.)., The Disabled Learner. Rotterdam University Press, Rotterdam.

Grossman, R. P. 1975. Attitudes about learning disabilities in Illinois: Private Schools, ACLD and the Universities. Chicago CPA 1974. Quoted in Senf, G. M., and Grossman, R. P. 1975. State initiative in learning disabilities: Illinois' Project SCREEN. J. Learn. Disabil. 8:587-596.

Grotberg, E. H. 1970. Neurological aspects of learning disabilities: A case for the disadvantaged. J. Learn. Disabil. 3:321-327.

Guralnick, M. J. 1973. A research-service model for the support of handicapped children. Except. Child. 39:277-282.

Halliwell, J. W., and Solan, H. A. 1972. The effects of a supplemental perceptional training program on reading achievement. Except. Child. 38:613-621.

Hammill, D. D., and Larsen, S. C. 1974. The effectiveness of psycholinguistic training. Except. Child. 41:5-14.

Harlow, H., and Harlow, M. K. 1949. Learning to think. Sci. Am. 181:36-39.

Haywood, H. C. 1976. Alternatives to normative assessment. Paper presented at the 4th Congress of the International Association for the Scientific Study of Mental Deficiency, Washington, D.C.

Hoffman, S. P., Engelhardt, D. M., Margolis, R. A., Polizos, P., Waizer, J., and Rosenfield, R. 1974. Response to methylphenidate in low socioeconomic children. Arch. Gen. Psychiat. 30:354–359.

Hunt, D. E. 1971. Matching models in education: The coordination of teaching methods with student characteristics. Monograph No. 10. Ontario Institute for Studies in Education, Toronto.

Hunt, J. McV. 1962. Intelligence and experience. The Ronald Press Company, New York.

Hutt, C., and Bhavnani, R. 1972. Predictions from play. Nature 237:171–172.

Jensen, A. R. 1969. How much can we boost IQ and scholastic achievement? In "Environment, Heredity and Intelligence." Reprint series No 2, Harvard Educational Review, pp. 1–123.

Jones, R. L. 1972. Labels and stigma in special education. Except. Child. 38:553–564.

Kamin, L. J. 1974. The science and politics of I.Q. Wiley, New York.

Keogh, B. K., and Becker, L. D. 1973. Early detection of learning problems: Questions, cautions, and guidelines. Except. Child. 40:5–11.

Keogh, B. K., and Smith, C. E. 1970. Early identification of educationally high and potentially high-risk children. J. Sch. Psychol. 8:285–290.

Lane, P. E. 1975. Editorial. J. Learn. Disabil. 8:473–475.

Larsen, S. C., and Hammill, D. D. 1975. The relationship of selected visual-perceptual abilities to school learning. J. Spec. Ed. 9:281–291.

Makins, V. 1976. Review of "Play: Its role in development and evolution" by J. S. Bruner, A. Volly, and K. Sylva in the *Times* Educational Supplement. June 4, 1976.

Marwit, S. J., and Stenner, A. J. 1972. Hyperkinesis: Delineation of two patterns. Except. Child. 38:401–406.

Maslow, A. 1955. Deficiency motivation and growth motivation. In M. R. Jones (ed.), Nebraska Symposium on Motivation, University of Nebraska Press, Lincoln, Nebraska.

Meichenbaum, D. H., and Goodman, J. 1971. Training impulsive children to talk to themselves: A means of developing self-control. J. Abnorm. Psychol. 77:115–126.

Murray, J. N. 1976. Is there a role for the teacher in the use of medication for hyperkinesis? J. Learn. Disabil. 9:30–35.

Myklebust, H. R., and Johnson, D. 1967. Learning disabilities: Educational principles and practices. Grune and Stratton, New York.

Neisworth, J. T., and Greer, J. G. 1975. Functional similarities of learning disability and mild retardation. Except. Child. 42:17–21.

Novak, H. S., Bonaventure, E., and Merenda, P. F. 1973. A scale for early detection of children with learning problems. Except. Child. 40:98–105.

O'Neill, M. J. 1975. An evaluation of a method for developing learning strategies in Kindergarten children with potential learning disabilities. Ph.D. Thesis, University of Toronto.

Overstreet, H. A. 1925. Influencing Human Behavior. W. W. Norton and Company, Inc., New York.

Pidgeon, D. A. 1970. Expectation and pupil performance. National Foundation for Educational Research, Slough, England.

Porteus, S. D., Barclay, J. E., Culver, H. S., and Kleman, J. P. 1960. Measurement of subconscious memory. Percept. Mot. Skills 10:215-229.

Reilly, V. V. 1970. Letter to the editor. Except. Child. 37:313-314.

Ross, A. O. 1976. Psychological aspects of learning disabilities and reading disorders. McGraw-Hill Book Company, New York.

Ross, D., and Ross, S. 1976. Hyperactivity. Wiley, New York.

Safer, D. J., and Allen, R. P. 1976. Hyperactive Children. University Park Press, Baltimore.

Samuels, S. J., and Turnure, J. E. 1974. Attention and reading in first-grade boys and girls. J. Educ. Psychol. 66:29-32.

Silberberg, N. E., and Silberberg, M. C. 1969. Myths in remedial education. J. Learn. Disabil. 2:209-217.

Stott, D. H. 1950. Delinquency and human nature. Carnegie U.K. Trust, Dunfermline, Fife.

Stott, D. H. 1959a. Evidence for prenatal impairment of temperament in mentally retarded children. Vita Humana 2:125-148.

Stott, D. H. 1959b. Infantile illness and subsequent mental and emotional development. J. Genet. Psychol. 94:233-251.

Stott, D. H. 1960. Observations on retest discrepancy in mentally subnormal children. Br. J. Educ. Psychol. 30:211-219.

Stott, D. H. 1961. I. Q. changes among educationally subnormal children. Spec. Educ. 50:11-14.

Stott, D. H. 1962. Programmed Reading Kit. Holmes McDougall, Edinburgh; Gage, Toronto; Scott Foresman, Chicago.

Stott, D. H. 1964. Roads to Literacy. Holmes McDougall, Edinburgh.

Stott, D. H. 1966. Commentary on "Genetic determination of differences in intelligence: A study of monozygotic twins reared together and apart," by Cyril Burt. Congenital influences on the development of twins. Brit. J. Psychol. 57:423-429.

Stott, D. H. 1970. The Flying Start Kit. Experimental pre-publication edition.

Stott, D. H. 1971. Flying Start Learning-to-learn Kits. Holmes McDougall, Edinburgh; Gage, Toronto. Distributed in the United States by University Park Press, Baltimore.

Stott, D. H. 1972. The Parent as Teacher. New Press, Toronto; Hodder and Stoughton, London; Fearon, Belmont, Calif.

Stott, D. H. 1973a. Follow-up study from birth of the effects of prenatal stresses. Develop. Med. Child Neurol. 15:770-787.

Stott, D. H. 1973b. Some less obvious cognitive aspects of learning to read. Reading Teacher. 26:374-383.

Stott, D. H. 1974. Manual to the Bristol Social Adjustment Guides. Hodder and Stoughton, London.

Stott, D. H. 1976. Pseudoretardation as a form of learning disability: The Case of Jean. J. Learn. Disabil. 9:354-364.

Stott, D. H. Developing learning capability in the retarded. J. Pract. Approach. Develop. Handicap. In press.

Stott, D. H., and Albin, J. 1975. Confirmation of a general factor of effectiveness-motivation by individual tests. Br. J. Educ. Psychol. 45:153–161.

Stott, D. H., and Latchford, S. A. 1976. Prenatal antecedents of child health and behavior: an epidemiological report of incidence and association. J. Am. Acad. Child Psychiat. 15:161–191.

Stott, D. H., and Marston, N. C. 1970. Bristol Social Adjustment Guides. Hodder and Stoughton, London.

Stott, D. H., Marston, N. C., and Neill, S. J. 1975. Taxonomy of behaviour disturbance. Hodder and Stoughton, London.

Stott, D. H., and Sharp, J. D. 1976. Scale of Effectiveness-Motivation. National Foundation for Educational Research, Slough, England.

Stott, D. H., Williams, H. L., and Sharp, J. D. 1976. Effectiveness-motivation in pre-school children. Educ. Res. 18:117–124.

Swanson, J. M., and Kinsbourne, M. 1976. Stimulant-related state-dependent learning in hyperactive children. Science 192:1354–1357.

Sylva, K., Bruner, J. S., and Genova, P. 1976. The role of play in the problem-solving of children 3–5 years old. In J. S. Bruner, K. Sylva, and P. Genova (eds.), Play: Its role in development and evolution. Penguin, Harmondsworth, Middlesex.

Vernon, M. D. 1957. Backwardness in Reading. Harvard University Press, Cambridge, Mass.

Vygotsky, L. S. 1962. Thought and Language. M. I. T. Press, Cambridge, Mass.

Walker, S. 1975. Drugging the American child: We've been too cavalier about hyperactivity. J. Learn. Disabil. 6:354–358.

Weithorn, C. J., and Ross, R. 1975. Who monitors medication? J. Learn. Disabil. 8:458–461.

White, R. W. 1959. Motivation reconsidered: The concept of competence. Psychol. Rev. 66:297–333.

Wilenski, R. H. 1927. The Modern Movement in Art, p. 196. Faber and Faber, London.

Zeaman, D., and House, B. J. 1963. The role of attention in retardate discrimination learning. In N. R. Ellis (ed.), Handbook of Mental Deficiency, pp. 159–223. McGraw-Hill, New York.

Zigler, E. 1966. Mental retardation: Current ideas and approaches. In L. W. Hoffman and M. Hoffman (eds.), Review of Child Development Research, Vol. II. Russell Sage Foundation, New York.

Zigler, E. 1970. Social class and the socialization process. Rev. Educ. Res. 40:87–110.

INDEX